THE WATCH

An illustrated guide to its
history and mechanism

THE WATCH

An illustrated guide to its
history and mechanism

JOHN CRONIN

THE CROWOOD PRESS

First published in 2022 by
The Crowood Press Ltd,
Ramsbury, Marlborough
Wiltshire SN8 2HR

enquiries@crowood.com

www.crowood.com

British Library Cataloguing-in-Publication Data
A catalogue record for this book is available from the British Library.

ISBN 978 0 7198 4088 3

Acknowledgements
The author would like to thank Pieces of Time London (www.antique-watch.com) for their kind permission to reproduce several watch photographs, and the staff of Knowsley Archive Service for their help with archive material. Staff at the Metropolitan Museum of Art in New York also need to be thanked for their enlightened attitude to copyright.

Disclaimer
Every reasonable effort has been made to track down the copyright holders of the images within. Please contact the publisher if an image has been credited incorrectly, and we will be happy to make amendments in any future edition.

Frontispiece
Cosimo I de' Medici, Duke of Florence, painted in 1560. The earliest known portrait featuring a watch. © *SCIENCE MUSEUM GROUP*

Typeset by Jean Cussons Typesetting, Diss, Norfolk
Cover design by Maggie Mellett
Printed and bound in India by Parksons Graphics

Contents

Introduction

Sometime in the fifteenth century, a new concept in timekeeping became possible: that of personal time. Measurement of the passage of time had come a long way since ancient civilizations had divided the day into twenty-four hours – twelve hours of daylight and twelve of night; these 'temporal hours' varied in length according to the seasons. The time-measuring devices available to the ancients, such as sundials and water clocks, could cope well enough with the simple demands of a period when the patterns of life were well adapted to the divisions of day and night.

Religious observance often involved prayers at certain times of the day. Jews were required to pray three times per day: in the morning, afternoon and evening, and worshippers were allowed a reasonably broad interpretation of the actual prayer times. Islam, however, was more demanding, requiring five daily prayers: at dawn, just after noon, before sunset, just after sunset and after dark. In Islamic countries, where the sun usually shines, sundials during daylight hours and simple water clocks sufficed to fix the times for religious obligations. As Christianity became organized, particularly with the establishment of monasteries, still more demands were made on the faithful. The rule of Benedict in the sixth century required seven daytime services and one at night.

It was believed that the 'second coming' would take place during the hours of darkness, and a night vigil, later known as Matins, became an essential element of life in a monastery. However, as the centuries passed, the timing of services tended to be left to individual houses, and by the eleventh century, the strict observance of monastic rules had often become less important than the pursuit of power and wealth.

The coming of the Cistercians, with their passion for order and strict discipline, changed all this, and in their new isolated monasteries they demanded a regular and punctual prayer cycle:

- Matins (during the night, at about 2am); also called Vigil
- Lauds or Dawn Prayer (at dawn, about 5am, but earlier in summer, later in winter)
- Prime or Early Morning Prayer (first hour, approximately 6am)
- Terce, or Mid-Morning Prayer (third hour, approximately 9am)
- Sext, or Midday Prayer (sixth hour, approximately 12 noon)

St Benedict – Fra Angelico.

- None, or Mid-Afternoon Prayer (ninth hour, approximately 3pm)
- Vespers, or Evening Prayer ('at the lighting of the lamps', about 6pm)
- Compline, or Night Prayer (before retiring, about 7pm)

Being late for worship was unthinkable, and bells controlled every aspect of the monk's life, including being awakened in the small hours of the night. Sounding the bell for Matins reliably must have been a matter of some anxiety for the Sacristan who was responsible. However, necessity is the father of invention, and the industrious and ingenious Cistercians solved the problem sometime in the thirteenth century with the invention of a mechanical timekeeper: this would sound an alarm to awaken the bell ringer to get the monks out of their beds at the appointed time. Unfortunately, none of these early clocks has survived, and dating them is confused by the use of the term 'horologium' (from the Greek *horologion*: time-teller) in monastic records, which could equally apply to

Salisbury Cathedral clock, fourteenth century: the earliest surviving mechanical timepiece.

other timekeepers, including sundials and water clocks.

The first detailed descriptions of clocks to come down to us are from the early fourteenth century; these were highly developed machines with striking works and complex astronomical dials. By this time, mechanical timepieces were well established in the great monasteries and churches of northern Europe. Tower clocks soon began to appear in large urban centres with bells striking the hours, regulating many aspects of urban life – particularly working times, the night watch and the opening and closing of town gates. These new clocks kept regular hours of equal length, and the old concept of temporal hours fell away in Europe – although some Eastern cultures, including the Japanese, held on to the old, irregular hours until the nineteenth century, and clocks were made with adjustable hour markers in an attempt to indicate the differing length of their hours.

By the fifteenth century the technology of wheel cutting had improved, and this made smaller domestic clocks possible for those who could afford to purchase them and pay the

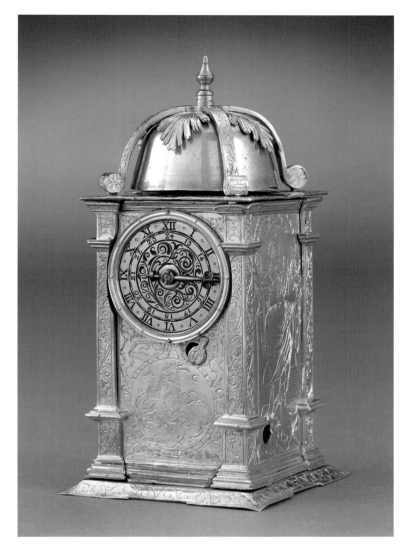

An early spring-driven German table clock, c.1570.

cost of maintenance. The power source for all these early clocks was the falling weight, which meant that they had to be firmly supported on some kind of framework, or hung from a wall. The possibility of having a clock that could be moved from room to room, or could accompany its owner when travelling, clearly had its attractions, and the search for a new power source began. The answer may have come from locksmiths, who had developed coiled springs for elaborate locks. The earliest clock springs may well have been made from hammered brass, and

they would need winding every few hours. Producing a thin ribbon of steel that could be coiled tightly without breaking was one of the great technological achievements of the fifteenth century, and made portable timekeeping a real possibility.

Around the end of the fifteenth century, spring clocks were being miniaturized to the extent that they were small enough to be carried around by the owner, either on a chain or in a purse (pockets were not yet a part of fashionable clothing). They were the wonder

Early portrait of unknown man with watch, 1577: Peter Paul Rubens.

of the age, and were objects of great status and conspicuous display, on which the arts of the jeweller and metalworker were lavished. The relative inaccuracy of these early watches was not a problem when the best source of time was a sundial. What the watch gave its privileged owner was a way of measuring the passage of the hours at any time of day or night, a source of personal time that would have marked the owner as a person of high status.

Where were these early watches produced? The oldest watch yet discovered dates from the early sixteenth century and was probably made in Augsburg. A certain Peter Henlein, a locksmith of Nürnberg, has been credited as the 'inventor' of a number of spring-driven devices in the early 1500s that could be described as watches, although none survives. There has also been speculation, based on very sketchy

evidence, that portable spring-driven timepieces were known in northern Italy in the 1490s. Another centre of early watchmaking was Blois in the Loire valley region of France. The common denominator in these places is that they were centres of patronage, where ingenious craftsmen were producing devices that would attract the attention of a wealthy clientèle willing to part with hard cash for the latest curiosities.

The two regions to emerge in the early sixteenth century as the main centres of watchmaking were what is now southern Germany, and France; however, the devastation caused by the Thirty Years' War (1618–1648) in German-speaking Europe meant that the focus of watch production moved west to France. As we will see, French ascendency was short-lived, as most French watchmakers were Huguenots and periodic religious persecution in France resulted in a large-scale emigration of skilled craftsmen to more sympathetic Protestant locations, including London and Geneva. For over two centuries, from around 1700, English watchmakers dominated the trade and were responsible for most technological advances, soon to be taken up in Switzerland and later in America, where modern mass production began.

In some ways the story of the development of the watch is comparable to the invention of the mobile telephone in recent times. The creation of modern telecommunications has happened at breakneck speed, and these devices that began as desirable objects for the few, spread to the poorest parts of the planet within a couple of decades. On the other hand, the story of the transformation of the watch from a status symbol for the rich and powerful to an everyday object spans half a millennium. Always at the cutting edge of technology and science, timekeepers were an essential element in the making of the modern world. This book sets out to give the general reader and collector a grasp of the key technological developments in the history of the mechanical watch, from its earliest manifestation as a high-status object for the super-rich, to the cheap, mass-produced timepieces of the twentieth century.

PART I:
THE DEVELOPMENT OF THE
WATCH MECHANISM

Drum watch. German, mid-sixteenth century.

Chapter 1
Early Watches: The Sixteenth to Seventeenth Centuries

The first portable mechanical devices that could be described as watches were probably made in northern Italy or southern Germany in the late fifteenth century. However, no watch from this period survives, and it is also possible that watch production began independently in France at the same time. The earliest written evidence we have (Johannes Cocleus' *Cosmographia Pomponii Melanie*, 1512) refers to a watchmaker named Peter Hele or Henlein, who made small timepieces that could be carried in a purse or pouch and ran for forty hours.

Possibly the earliest surviving watch is dated 1530 and can be seen at the Walters Art Museum, Baltimore: it is a small spherical timepiece in gilt brass 48mm in diameter, and is engraved with the owner's name: Phillip Melanchthon. He was a German Protestant reformer and

Pommander watch c.1530: attributed to Peter Henlein, Augsburg. WALTERS MUSEUM BALTIMORE

Peter Henlein watch detail.

1526,
VIVENTIS·POTVIT·DVRERIVS·ORA·PHILIPPI
MENTEM·NON·POTVIT·PINGERE·DOCTA
MANVS

Portrait of Phillip Melanchthon.

collaborator of Martin Luther in Augsburg. It has no maker's name, but it would seem likely that it was made there. The only other similar survival from this period is a spherical watch now in the Ashmolean Museum, Oxford. Watchmaker guilds were established in Augsburg and Nuremberg in the 1560s, and most of the earliest known watches come from this region.

Most of these early watches were drum-shaped and were developed from larger spring-driven table clocks that appeared in the late 1400s; they were a triumph of late medieval technology, and resulted from two centuries

Sixteenth-century German drum watch.

Drum watch, Christopher Schisster Augsberg.

of innovation in horology. The earliest known painting featuring a watch is a portrait, believed to be of Cosimo I de Medici, Duke of Florence, painted in 1560; he is shown holding a drum-shaped watch with a pierced lid and single hand, with a key attached to a silk ribbon. The watch is carefully painted, and on a nearby table is a three-legged object that appears to incorporate a bell; it has been suggested that this was an alarm device that could be attached to the watch. The Duke is shown at the height of his power as ruler of Florence, and graphically illustrates the importance of such watches as status symbols.

Cosimo I de' Medici. © *SCIENCE MUSEUM GROUP*

Chapter 2
The Elements of Construction

To understand these timepieces we need to look at the construction of the first clocks.

All mechanical timepieces consist of three main elements: a power source, a gear train, and a time controller and escapement.

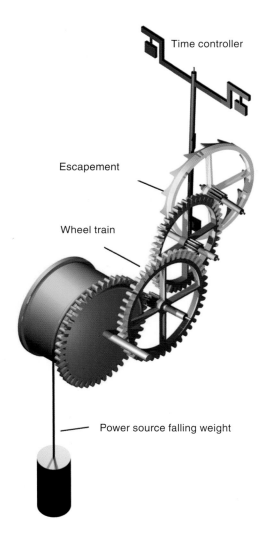

The layout of the early clock.

POWER SOURCE

The Falling Weight

The force of gravity powered the first mechanical clocks developed at some time in the thirteenth century. The weight was generally attached to a rope that wound round a barrel; the barrel was attached to a wheel (the 'great wheel') through a ratchet, allowing the barrel to turn and wind up the weight. Weights provided early clocks with a more or less steady and unvarying source of power; the only drawback was that they needed to be supported on a fixed platform to work. This was fine when clocks were built in towers or firmly fixed to a wall bracket; however, as smaller timepieces were developed for domestic use in the early fifteenth century, a tantalizing and highly commercial possibility emerged: the portable timepiece.

By the early 1400s the clock had moved from a device primarily designed to sound an alarm to awaken monks for the observation of the night-time office of Matins, to tower clocks sounding the bells that marked the passing of the hours in urban centres. These mechanisms were made from iron, using technology developed by the blacksmith; steel, much harder and with great potential for higher precision components, was difficult and expensive to make and was confined mainly to the production of weapons, knives and other cutting tools.

By the fifteenth century, smaller domestic clocks rapidly became status symbols in wealthy households, and the manufacture of these timepieces quickly spread throughout Europe. As these symbols of wealth were confined to a fixed place in the owner's house, an obvious development would be to make the clock portable so that not only could it be moved from room to room, but it could also accompany the owner when travelling. But to make this possible, a new source of power was needed.

The Coiled Spring

The spring was one of the earliest inventions of humanity – prehistoric hunters well understood the capacity of the bow to store the energy of the arm and release it to propel an arrow. By 1400 metal springs were used in all kinds of devices and weapons. One of the outstanding technological achievements of the period was the invention, probably by locksmiths, of a spring that could be coiled in such a way that it could be 'wound up' to store energy that, when released, would provide several turns of rotary motion.

By the mid-fifteenth century, spring-powered domestic clocks began to appear; none of the earliest springs has survived, but they were probably made from a strip of hammered brass. Brass can be 'work hardened' by hammering to make it more elastic than in its cast state. These early springs could only have powered the clock for short periods, and probably needed winding twice a day. Iron was too brittle to be used to make springs; however, if iron is alloyed with a small percentage of carbon, it makes steel, which can be worked in its soft state, then hardened and tempered by heating and quenching the metal to make it resilient and flexible.

Before the seventeenth century, steel was mostly used for the production of weapons and other cutting tools. Wootz steel – iron with a carbon content of around 1.5 per cent – originated in India and was widely exported to Europe and the Middle East in pre-Christian times, where it was often known as Damascus steel. Swords made from Damascus steel became highly prized for their strength and elastic properties; it was possible to bend one of these swords through 90 degrees without it breaking. Early spring makers would have used the techniques of the swordsmith to hammer out a thin ribbon of steel, which would be hardened and tempered before it was coiled and enclosed in a barrel.

The outer coil of the spring is attached to a hook on the inside of the barrel, and the inner coil is hooked to the barrel arbor; the arbor

Barrel lid

Barrel arbor

Mainspring

Spring barrel

Mainspring components.

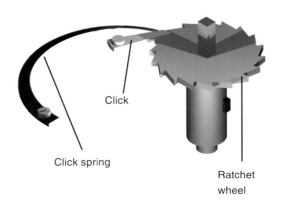

Click

Click spring

Ratchet wheel

The ratchet.

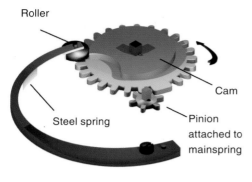

Roller

Steel spring

Cam

Pinion attached to mainspring

Mainspring fully wound

Mainspring running down

The stackfreed.

has a square section that allows the spring to be wound with a key. The square on the arbor also holds the ratchet wheel, which prevents the spring from running down.

The problem with using a coiled spring as a power source is that as it runs down, it provides progressively less power (torque). This variation in power would result in poor timekeeping, and some form of compensation was needed to lessen this effect. It appears that the problem was tackled very soon after the introduction of spring-driven timepieces in the first half of the fifteenth century, with two inventions: the stackfreed and the fusee.

The Stackfreed

The stackfreed probably originated in southern Germany, and was particularly suited to smaller timepieces as it was very compact. 'Stackfreed' probably comes from the German *starken feder* (strong spring). The spring pushes on a cam geared to the mainspring; when the watch is fully wound the roller presses hard against the cam and the resulting friction lessens the power of the mainspring; as the watch runs down, the roller pushes on the smaller diameter of the cam, producing less friction as the mainspring

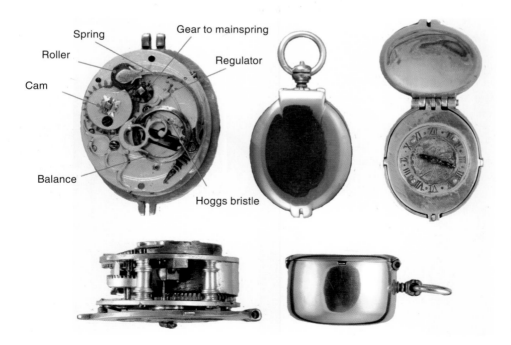

Spring

Gear to mainspring

Roller

Regulator

Cam

Balance

Hoggs bristle

Stackfreed watch — German, late sixteenth century.
PIECES OF TIME

runs down, and tending to even out the changing power output.

An additional function of the gearing is that the wheel attached to the cam has a blanked-out tooth, which locks the mainspring before it becomes fully wound or entirely run down. This device is called a stop-work, and it limits the mainspring to around four turns, avoiding using the fully wound and near run-down portions of the spring when the power variation would be at its greatest.

The Fusee

The fusee was a much more sophisticated device that may have originated in a type of tapered windlass used to tension powerful crossbows. A normal windlass was a cylinder turned with levers, round which a rope was wound. If the cylinder was replaced with a cone, then the pulling power would be increased as the rope wound round the narrower part of the cone, providing extra torque as the tension of the bow increased.

The spring is wound from the fusee by a gut line wound round the mainspring barrel; as

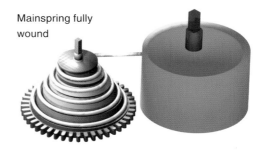

Mainspring fully wound

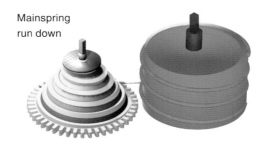

Mainspring run down

Mainspring and fusee.

French early seventeenth-century watch with fusee.
PIECES OF TIME

the line is wound on to the fusee, the mainspring is tensioned. When the mainspring is fully wound, the fusee line pulls on the narrow section of the cone. As the spring runs down, it pulls on progressively larger sections of the fusee cone, gradually increasing the torque to the gear train, compensating for the decreasing power of the spring.

Not all the turns of the spring are used; when the fusee is run down, the mainspring is still under power so that the last turn or so is not used. Likewise, when the fusee is fully wound, the spring in the barrel still has a turn or so of winding left. This avoids the coils of the spring in the barrel becoming tightly pressed together, giving a smoother release of power. The system can also be 'set up' by varying the number of turns the spring is given when the fusee becomes run down, giving a little more or less power.

The fusee was one of the most ingenious devices of the period, and it became an essential component of all precision spring-driven timepieces. Horologists soon learned that by closely matching the shape of the fusee to the properties of the mainspring, it was possible to eliminate almost all variations in torque. However, one of the problems that plagued early watchmakers was that thin gut lines tended to break; this was solved by developing fine steel fusee chains, although gut line continued to be used successfully in larger clocks.

GEAR TRAIN

Early Use of Gearing

The use of gears long pre-dates the first clocks — we know of complex gear systems from ancient Greece, and in 1901, an object was discovered in an ancient shipwreck off the coast of the Greek island of Antikythera, which transformed our knowledge of ancient mechanics. It consists of eighty-two crust-encased fragments of a bronze mechanism and the remains of a wooden box; at that time, the purpose of this machine was a mystery. However, with the aid of modern x-ray techniques it has been possible to reconstruct the instrument with its complex gearing, consisting of over thirty-seven bronze gear wheels, the largest of which is 13cm in diameter, with 223 teeth. The gears are turned with a handwheel, while various dials with pointers can be used to predict astronomical positions and eclipses in future decades, based on the calculations of the second century BC astronomer Hipparchus of Rhodes.

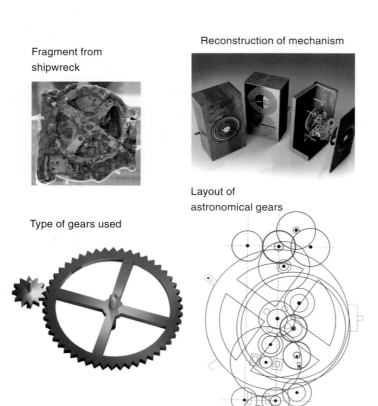

Fragment from shipwreck

Reconstruction of mechanism

Type of gears used

Layout of astronomical gears

Antikythera mechanism, first century BC.

Reconstruction of Giovani de Dondi's mid-fourteenth-century astronomical clock.

The chance discovery of such advanced use of gearing for mathematical calculations gives us a tantalizing glimpse into Greek engineering. It reveals a technology that was not equalled until the European renaissance, when astronomical clocks first appeared capable of predicting the positions of the sun, moon and planets, together with tides and religious feast days. Whilst these early clocks no longer exist, detailed descriptions survive, including one by the mathematician Richard of Wallingford in St Albans during the 1330s. Another from the mid-fourteenth century by Giovani de Dondi of Padua had seven dials and 107 moving parts. Using a description of de Dondi's clock, it has been possible to make a convincing working reconstruction.

The Evolution of Horological Gearing

Two or more gears working in sequence are known as a 'gear train'; in mechanical timepieces, a gear train has the dual purpose of transmitting the energy from the weight or spring to the escapement, and transferring the beats of the time controller (for example, a pendulum) to the hands indicating the time.

In medieval times simple gearing, generally made of wood, was commonly found in various types of mill, transferring water or wind power to drive pumps and grindstones.

The earliest reference to 'segmental gears' – circular gears with peripheral teeth – comes from the Islamic scholar and engineer Ismail al Jazari (1136–1206) in his *Book of the knowledge of ingenious mechanical devices* of 1206, which describes fifty mechanical devices with instructions for building them. His drawing of a water pump from this book, together with a modern reconstruction, is included.

Early clocks generally used a combination

ABOVE: *Cage gearing.*

BELOW: *Al Jazera manuscript and reconstruction.*

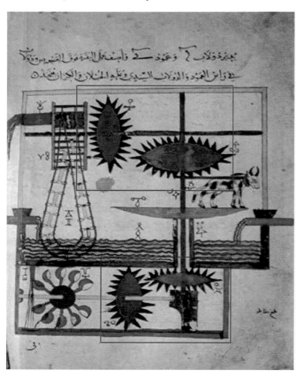

Lantern pinion

Contrate wheel

Wheel crossings

Pinnion

ABOVE: *Spur gearing.*

LEFT: *Early gears.*

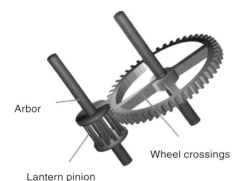

Arbor

Wheel crossings

Lantern pinion

of 'spur gears' – wheels with peripheral teeth – and lantern pinions. The wheel teeth would be marked out with dividers and filed out by hand; the smaller pinions were made by inserting forged iron rods into a cage. This can be clearly seen in the fourteenth-century Salisbury Cathedral clock illustrated in the introduction.

As wheel cutting improved, it became possible to cut even teeth in brass wheel blanks accurately, and spur gearing replaced lantern pinions. As a result, the combination of brass wheel gearing with steel pinions became almost universal in horological gearing, and has stood the test of time: well-made gear trains have given over 300 years of service with little sign of wear.

By the seventeenth century, sophisticated machinery had been developed to cut wheels accurately. The machine illus-

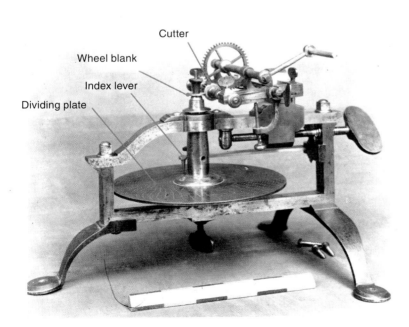

Cutter

Wheel blank

Index lever

Dividing plate

Eighteenth-century wheel-cutting machine.

trated has a rotating dividing plate with circular rows of holes for various wheel counts – the index lever locks the plate in position whilst a tooth is cut, then the plate is moved round for the next tooth. When the teeth were all cut, the blank could then be moved to a similar machine for rounding off – that is, finishing the tips of the teeth. Horological wheels were always 'crossed out' to lighten the wheel, reducing its inertia; this was done by hand sawing and filing.

TIME CONTROLLER AND ESCAPEMENT

A time controller regulates the speed at which the gear train moves forwards; it is driven by an escapement that gives periodic impulses to maintain its motion. The first clocks used a foliot: this was a horizontal bar caused to swing in alternate directions by a verge escapement. The

invention of the escapement in the thirteenth century was the key to producing the first truly mechanical timekeeper. Its origin is unknown, although it has been suggested that it may have been developed from earlier devices used to ring bells.

The foliot is driven in alternate directions by the action of the escape-wheel teeth on the pallets of the verge. The drawing shows the foliot being operated by the escape wheel. The action of the escapement is as follows:

1. As the escape wheel rotates, a tooth pushes the entry pallet in an anti-clockwise direction.
2. The wheel continues and is locked on the exit pallet by the opposing tooth, pushing it in a clockwise direction.
3. The escape wheel then locks again on the entry pallet.

Thus, the rocking motion of the escapement bar maintains the approximately 60-degree to-and-fro swing of the foliot. (It is possible to find an on-line animation to make this clearer.)

The time taken by each swing can be adjusted by moving weights inwards or outwards along the bar, given a fairly constant power source provided by a falling

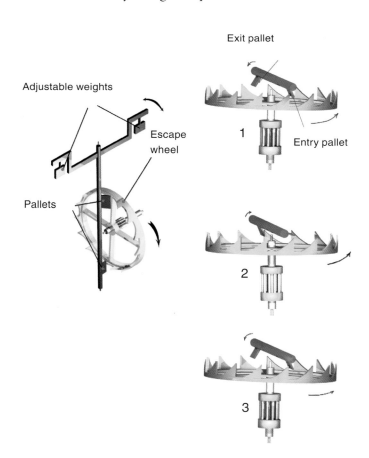

Verge escapement with foliot balance.

weight and careful adjustment; timekeeping of a few minutes per day is possible with these clocks. Greater accuracy had to wait for the introduction of the pendulum in the late seventeenth century.

In the mid-fifteenth century, the first portable timepieces used a simple bar balance similar to the foliot but without the adjustable weights; the balance wheel soon replaced this. To give some measure of adjustment, the arms of the balance wheel were made to bounce off a pair of hog's bristles mounted on a pivoted lever. The lever could be moved towards or away from the centre of the wheel; this increased or decreased the angle through which the wheel rotated, causing a gaining or losing rate.

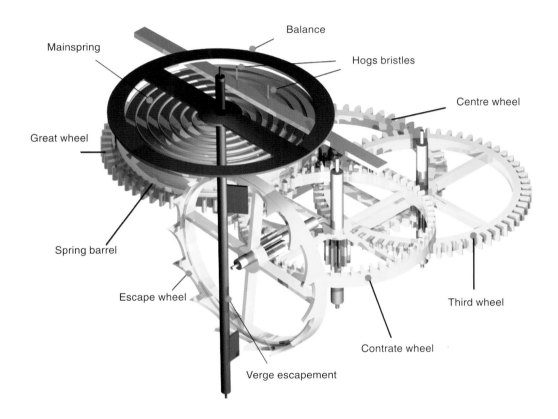

Verge escapement with a hog's bristle controller.

Chapter 3
Eighteenth-Century Improvements

THE BALANCE SPRING

A revolutionary improvement in the timekeeping of watches came with the introduction of the balance spring (often called the hairspring) in the late seventeenth century. The invention of this vitally important innovation was disputed at the time. The Dutch scientist Christiaan Huygens (1629–1695), who first adapted the pendulum to a clock mechanism, claimed to have invented the balance spring: he published a drawing in 1675 showing a spring attached to a watch balance, although the drawing of the escapement is inaccurate.

The great English scientist Robert Hooke (1635–1703) was the first to formulate the prop-

erties of the spring: in 1660 he produced *Hooke's Law*, which states that the extension of a spring is in direct proportion to the load applied to it. When a spiral spring was applied to the watch balance, the action of the spring had a profound effect on the rate. As the balance oscillated, it had a strong influence over the time taken for each turn of the wheel. The rate could now be controlled by the strength of the spring, rather than just the inertia of the wheel.

Huygens tried to obtain a royal patent on the device; he also sent a claim as to his priority for the invention to the Royal Society in early 1675. When Hooke heard about this, he immediately made a counterclaim and produced a watch, probably made for him by Thomas Tompion,

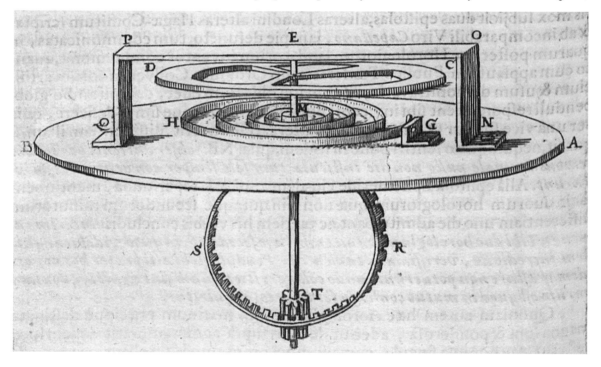

Huygens' drawing of 1675 showing a balance wheel with spring attached.

Christiaan Huygens.

Portrait of a mathematician, believed to be of Robert Hooke.

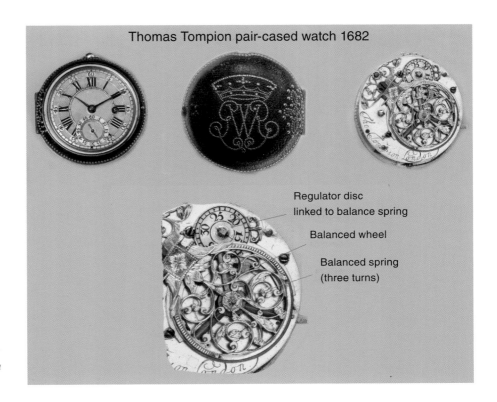

The Tompion watch (Museum of Modern Art, New York).

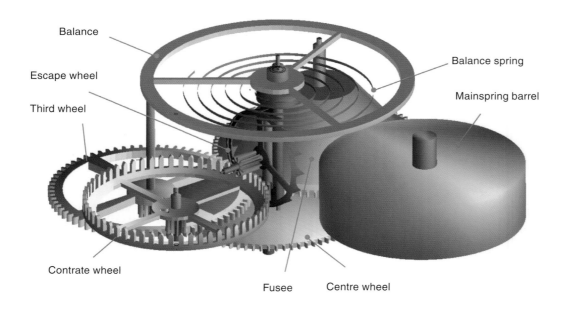

Balance

Escape wheel

Third wheel

Balance spring

Mainspring barrel

Contrate wheel

Fusee   Centre wheel

Typical layout of late seventeenth-century verge watch.

the great English clock and watchmaker, some years earlier. Unfortunately this watch has not survived, and numerous vague contemporary descriptions of watches with springs attached to the balance spring are inconclusive.

The Metropolitan Museum of Arts, New York, does have an extraordinary pair-cased watch by Tompion from 1682, which has a balance spring of three turns and a regulator; it also has a seconds hand, a most unusual feature at that time. Tompion's earliest balance-spring watches dispensed with the fusee; Huygens had suggested that it was no longer necessary, however, Tompion soon reconsidered, and his design with the fusee became the standard pattern for the next century.

Whether the idea of the balance spring came first from Hooke or Huygens, or both, is still undecided, but Tompion certainly played a central

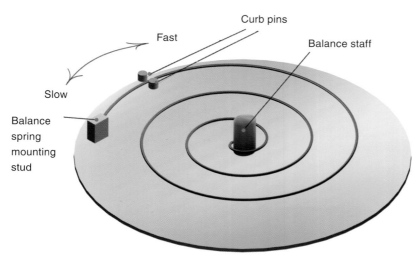

Curb pins

Fast

Balance staff

Slow

Balance spring mounting stud

Disc holding curb pin geared to regulator

Balance spring with regulator.

role in the success of the new design. All earlier single-handed watches were now obsolete, because instead of timekeeping of half an hour or so per day, balance-spring watches would go to within a few minutes per day, which justified the inclusion of a minute hand.

REGULATING

To regulate the timekeeping of the balance with a balance spring, a rotating disc was placed underneath the spring with two pins, called curb pins, placed on either side of the outer coil of the spring; as the spring wound and unwound, the curb pins limited the effective length of the spring. As the disc was rotated, the curb pins moved along the spring, effectively shortening and lengthening it, causing a losing or gaining rate.

This type of regulator was introduced by Tompion, who fitted it to his watches from around 1680; he used a plate geared to the rotating disc inscribed with numbers to make the adjustment easier. This type of regulator was quickly adopted by other makers, and remained in use until the early nineteenth century.

WATCH JEWELS

Watch wheels turned on pivots in bearings, which were simply holes in the brass plates. Over the years these bearing holes would wear into an oval shape due to the side pressure of the wheel. This caused the wheel to move slightly out of position, resulting in the gear teeth moving apart and not engaging properly: this reduced the power transmitted by the wheel train, causing the watch to stop.

The solution was to use a much harder material for the bearings, which could be highly pol-

Watch jewels. Top: *a ruby jewel bearing;* middle: *a wheel pivot running in a jewel hole;* bottom: *a capped bearing with endstone used for balance wheels.*

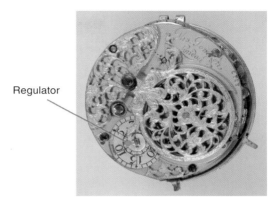
Regulator

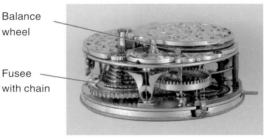
Balance wheel
Fusee with chain

Two views of the late 17th-century Tompion watch, showing his regulator. Also, note the new-style steel chain winding round the fusee.

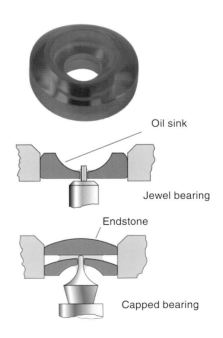
Oil sink
Jewel bearing
Endstone
Capped bearing

ished, reducing friction and wear. The use of ruby for watch bearings was first proposed by Nicholas Facio (1664–1753), a Swiss mathematician and astronomer who settled in England in 1687. He became a protégé of Isaac Newton, and was elected to the Royal Society in 1668; in 1704 he was granted a patent for watches with jewelled bearings.

The techniques of drilling and shaping watch jewels remained in England for most of the eighteenth century, giving the London makers a considerable advantage over continental rivals. By 1750 all quality English-made watches included jewel bearings for the balance wheel, and increasingly for the train wheels. Specially shaped jewels were later used for escapement parts as well as bearings. The invention of synthetic ruby at the end of the nineteenth century made watch jewels considerably cheaper, enabling them to be used in modestly priced mass-produced watches.

These improvements resulted in an increase in accuracy from perhaps a quarter of an hour per day to a minute or two per day, which was more than adequate when accurate time was not generally available.

WINDING AND HAND SETTING

Motion Work

As watches improved, the single hour hand for indicating the time of day became obsolete. During the early seventeenth century the minute hand became increasingly common in clocks, and later in the century watchmakers were also adopting the same refinement. Driving the two hands involved a set of gears known as the 'motion work' to synchronize both hands, and a friction device to allow the hands to be turned without disturbing the rest of the mechanism.

Early watches were constructed with a wheel that turned every twelve hours, and it was a simple matter to attach the single-hand friction tight to this wheel. With the addition of the minute hand, a more advanced method of providing friction between the centre wheel and the hands was required. The diagram shows the centre wheel (that turns once per hour), which has a hole drilled through the arbor. The friction shaft fits loosely through this hole but was given a kink at its centre so that when pushed into the centre arbor it held firmly but could be turned to adjust the hands. The minute pinion holds the

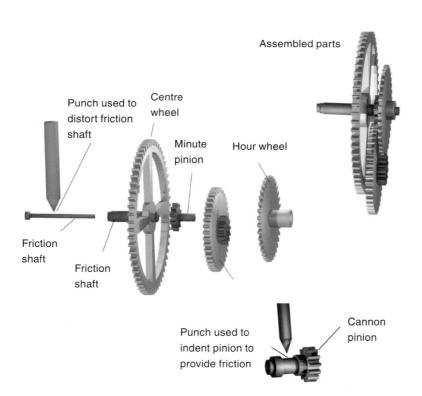

The motion work and friction drive.

minute hand and fits tightly on this shaft when the watch is assembled.

Two more wheels are required to complete the motion work: the hour wheel, which fits over the minute pinion and carries the hour hand, and a minute wheel that gears with the minute pinion and the hour wheel. The three wheels together provide the 1:12 reduction required to keep the two hands in step.

The Cannon Pinion

Towards the end of the nineteenth century, a new device to provide friction was gradually adopted. The cannon pinion made it easier to adjust the hand friction and to dismantle the watch for servicing. This replaced the earlier minute pinion and friction shaft, and was pushed over the centre-wheel arbor, which was extended to carry the minute hand. To provide the correct degree of friction for setting the hands, a punch is applied to a small indent that grips the centre-wheel arbor. The rest of the motion work was unchanged. This design continues to the present day.

Keyless Work

Before the late nineteenth century, watches were generally wound with a key, which was

also used to set the hands. Setting the hands required the owner to open the bezel holding the glass to expose the dial and hands; the key was then located on to a square to which the minute hand was attached, and turned to adjust the time. With the development of more delicate watches this process was rather risky, and to avoid damage a keyless system was needed to both wind the watch and set the hands.

The rocking-bar system was very commonly used in the late nineteenth and early twentieth centuries, and can be found in most English Lever watches. The winding crown turns the winding stem, which is attached to the contrate

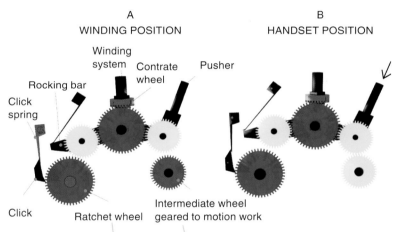

Rocking-bar keyless work.

wheel; this is geared via an intermediate wheel (blue) to the two wheels mounted on the rocking bar. The drawing 'A' shows the left-hand wheel geared to the ratchet wheel (connected to the mainspring); when the winding stem is turned the mainspring is wound. To set the hands the push-piece is depressed, moving the rocking bar clockwise, breaking the connection with the ratchet wheel and engaging the motion work. Whilst the push-piece is depressed, the hands can be turned either way; when the push-piece is released, the rocking bar springs back into the winding position, demonstrated in drawing 'B'.

Shifting Sleeve Keyless Work

This is essentially the modern keyless system and was popularized by American makers in the second half of the nineteenth century. The main parts are a pair of interlocking wheels, the clutch wheel, and the winding pinion. The clutch wheel has a square hole and the winding pinion a round hole, and they fit together so that the ratchet teeth on both wheels engage each other.

The winding stem is a shaft on which the two wheels are assembled. The illustration shows the winding stem to which the winding crown is attached. 'A' shows the assembly in the handset position: the winding pinion and clutch wheel are disengaged, and the clutch wheel has moved along the stem square to gear with the motion work. 'B' shows the winding position: the clutch wheel has moved along the stem to engage with the winding pinion, and the two wheels lock together with the stem to wind the mainspring.

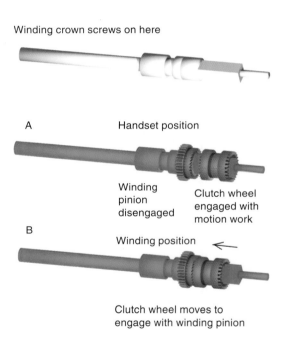

Winding crown screws on here

A　　Handset position

Winding pinion disengaged

Clutch wheel engaged with motion work

B

Winding position

Clutch wheel moves to engage with winding pinion

The winding stem assembly.

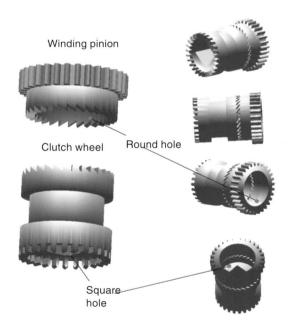

Winding pinion

Clutch wheel　　Round hole

Square hole

Clutch wheel and winding pinion.

The rest of the keyless work is a series of levers that move the clutch wheel up and down the stem. The set lever has a stud that locks into the winding stem: 'A' shows the stem pulled out into the handset position; 'B' shows how the set lever rotates when the stem is pushed in: it operates the clutch lever, which moves the clutch wheel to engage the winding pinion — the system is now in the winding position. Note that the ratchet teeth on the winding pinion and clutch wheel allow winding in one direction and free-wheeling in the other; the clutch lever spring keeps the two wheels engaged.

'C' shows the rest of the parts that complete the keyless work. The set lever spring (also called the cover plate) has two notches that engage with a pin on the set lever; this locks the set lever in one of its two positions as the stem is pulled in and out. Two gear wheels link the clutch assembly to the mainspring and motion work. In the handset position (left), the clutch wheel operates the motion work to set the hands; the winding pinion with its round hole does not turn with the stem. In the winding position (right), when the stem is pushed in, the clutch wheel moves down the square part of the stem and engages with the winding pinion.

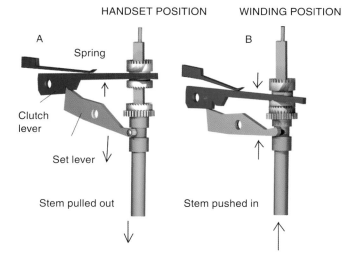

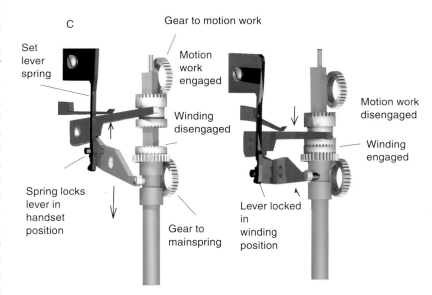

Keyless operation.

Chapter 4
The Seventeenth to Eighteenth Centuries: The Age of Decoration

Gold and enamel watch — Richard Gregg, London 1723.

WATCHMAKING IN LONDON

In the late seventeenth century, the European centre of watchmaking moved to London; after the restoration of Charles II and the 'Glorious Revolution' of 1688, England was at peace and emerging as the great world power it would become by the late eighteenth century. The Thirty Years' War, from 1618 to 1648, was one of the most destructive periods in European history; northern Europe and the Low Countries were impoverished, including the great watchmaking centres.

In France, the protestant Huguenots were being persecuted, and around 200,000 fled to England, Holland and Scandinavia. Many of these were superb horological craftsmen who found a warm welcome in London, training a whole generation of English makers, including Daniel Quare and Thomas Tompion, who was later known as the 'father' of English clockmaking. The Worshipful Company of Clockmakers was founded in 1631; they organized the London trade and did much to establish its reputation for quality work (they have a fine collection on display in London's Science Museum — a must for all collectors).

Bushman watch. © *THE BRITISH MUSEUM*

An example of continental watchmakers working in London at this time is John Bushman, born Johannes Buschmann III, son of Johannes Buschmann II of Augsburg. In his late twenties, he travelled to London via The Hague and is recorded as working there in 1690. The British Museum has a silver pair cased watch *c.* 1700 signed 'Bushman London'; it is particularly interesting as it has a portrait bust of King William III on the dial and the English royal coat of arms on the balance cock; what could be more English?

WATCH GLASSES

Early watches had a cover to protect the dial and hand, and this would be lifted to tell the time. Some of these watches had the cover made from transparent rock crystal (quartz) so that the dial was always visible. The technique of making lenses for eye glasses was well established by the end of the sixteenth century, and it would have been a small step to glaze watch cases, which probably began around 1610. Early glasses were probably cut from blown glass spheres using a red-hot iron ring, then ground to shape.

Later in the century a method was developed using moulds of different shapes according to the depth of dome required. A sheet of glass was placed over the mould, and a stone shaped to the inner dimensions of the glass was placed on top; when the mould was heated in an oven, the glass, under the weight of the stone, sank into the mould and could then be ground to shape.

THE PAIR CASED WATCH

Most watches made from the late seventeenth century to the early nineteenth century used a similar case design – this comprised an inner case that contained the movement and dial, protected by an outer hinged case with a push-button release. The outer case was often highly decorated both inside and out, and it had to be removed in order to expose the inner case with the winding hole into which the key was inserted. The hands were generally set with the same key, usually by lifting the hinged bezel that held

the glass, and locating the key on to the square in the centre of the minute hand.

The outer cases of these watches were often highly decorated, many with engraved or repoussé work where the metal was punched out from behind.

Exotic materials such as tortoiseshell and shagreen (made from the skin of sharks or rays) were often used with inlay work.

Pair cased watch by Tompion, late seventeenth century.

Gold repoussé watch case – Wm Webster 1723.
PIECES OF TIME

For watches of the highest value, various forms of enamel work were used. Early watches used the 'basse taille' technique, in which the artist creates a low-relief pattern in silver or gold, which is then decorated by chasing or engraving. The entire pattern is created in such

Silver tortoiseshell case, late seventeenth century; CH Godfrey. PIECES OF TIME

a way that its highest point is lower than the surrounding metal. Translucent enamel is then applied to the metal, allowing light to reflect from the relief, creating an attractive effect.

By the early seventeenth century, the city of Blois had become the centre of French goldsmithing and enamelling, and under the patronage of the royal family and aristocracy, workshops were established there, which revolutionized the art.

Around 1640, Jean and Henri Toutin developed a technique of painting in enamel that was soon applied to watch case decoration. They were able to produce miniature paintings of astonishing detail and vibrant colour, which could be handled without risk of damage. The skills needed were formidable, as each colour (made from powdered glass) melts at a different temperature; the painter had to apply the colours one at a time, and the work was then heated to the precise temperature that caused it to fuse to the level below; this was repeated for

Shagreen-cased watch, late seventeenth century.

French mid-eighteenth-century watch signed 'Musson' with basse taille enamelling.

Late sixteenth-century enamellers' workshop.

each colour as the picture was built up. At each stage in the process there was a risk of air bubbles being trapped in the enamel, which would cause the whole work to be ruined.

As the art of enamel painting spread to other countries, the price (and generally the quality) of these cases fell considerably. Swiss makers began producing enamelled cases in large quantities by the late eighteenth century.

Painted enamel watch case by Nicholas Gribelin, c.1680.

Swiss painted enamel watch case, c.1780.

Chapter 5
The Quest for Precision

IMPROVEMENTS IN THE ESCAPEMENT

From the latter part of the seventeenth century, astronomers were able to establish the time accurately by observing the movement of stars across a fixed point. In the early eighteenth century pendulum clocks were developed for use in observatories that were capable of keeping time to a second or so per month. However, there was no real incentive to improve the timekeeping of watches, and accuracy of a minute or two per day was considered quite adequate. We must remember that there was no standard time across the country until the coming of the railways, and watches and clocks would be set to local time, which varied by several minutes per day east and west of London.

Watchmaker, eighteenth-century print.

THE CYLINDER ESCAPEMENT

Timekeeping was somewhat improved with the development of the cylinder escapement by George Graham around 1726, from original experiments by his friend and partner Thomas Tompion. This was an advance over the verge escapement as it allowed the balance wheel to rotate further between impulses from the escapement.

Whilst it was an advance on the old verge escapement, it still had the drawback that it

Escape wheel tooth rests on inside surface of cylinder

Cylinder rotates anticlockwise, escape wheel tooth is released to give impulse

Cylinder continues to rotate, escape wheel tooth locks on outside of cylinder

Cylinder reverses direction and tooth pushes cylinder clockwise

Find an online animation to make the action clearer

Cylinder escapement.

Early nineteenth-century repeating watch by Breguet with ruby cylinder. PIECES OF TIME

the early nineteenth century French and Swiss makers favoured the escapement, producing thin, elegant watches, and later in the century, Swiss makers mass produced small cylinder fob watches for women in huge numbers.

THE DUPLEX ESCAPEMENT

Several other frictional rest escapements appeared during the eighteenth century. One worth mentioning was the duplex invented by

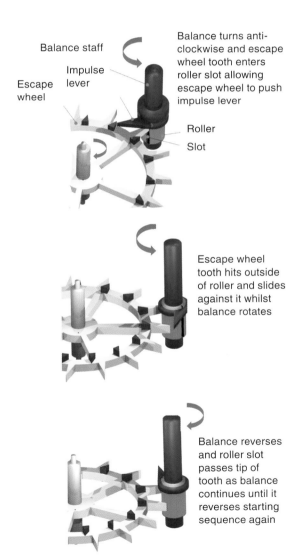

The duplex escapement.

was a frictional rest escapement – the escape wheel is in continual contact with the balance. The holy grail of escapement design was the detached escapement, where the balance is free to turn without friction apart from when it receives its impulse.

Cylinders were later made from ruby in an attempt to improve performance; however, the escapement was expensive to produce and was confined to higher priced watches, and it failed to replace the old verge escapement, which continued in use well into the nineteenth century. Nevertheless, the cylinder escapement did have the advantage of being very compact, making smaller, slimmer watches possible. In

Pierre Le Roy, which became popular for a while in England in the early nineteenth century. This escapement worked in a similar way to the cylinder, but the impulse was in one direction only – separating the locking and impulse actions allowed the balance to rotate through a larger arc. However, the balance was still not free, and the friction of the escape wheel against the roller affected the timekeeping.

SEA CLOCKS AND THE LONGITUDE PROBLEM

The development of sea clocks stimulated the next series of advances in watch design. The extreme difficulty in making portable timepieces capable of performing accurately at sea set a challenge that occupied inventors for the best part of a century. The result was a golden age in horology when staggering advances were made, transforming the watch from an object confirming its owner's wealth and status to a serious scientific instrument capable of playing a vital part in the emerging modern world.

The lack of an accurate method of navigation resulted in enormous losses of shipping before the late eighteenth century. It was a serious impediment to trade, particularly to maritime nations such as Britain with its growing overseas empire.

Navigation at sea requires two map coordinates to be determined: latitude and longitude. Latitude – that is, the north/south position – was easily found by measuring the angle of the sun or a fixed star above the horizon. However, longitude, the east/west position, was much more difficult, and could only be guessed at by dead reckoning – an estimate of how far the ship had travelled east or west.

The great maritime powers urgently needed a practical solution to the longitude problem, and offered a cash prize to anyone who could contribute to finding the answer in the hope that this might concentrate minds. As far back as 1598, Phillip III of Spain, at a time when memories of the disaster of the Armada were still fresh, offered a generous pension and large cash payment to 'the discoverer of longitude'. Considerable sums were advanced to encourage anyone who showed promise of making progress. It is hardly surprising that the Escorial was besieged by a stream of con artists and lunatics, as well as serious inventors. However, after many years of fruitless investigation and considerable expenditure, the Spanish government lost interest and the search was abandoned.

Holland, France, Venice and Great Britain all followed the same route, together with private individuals offering generous prizes for the elusive solution. The largest and best known was the British scheme. In 1714, Parliament set up a committee that consulted a number of eminent men, including Newton and Halley. Newton's evidence is worth quoting:

> ...for determining the longitude at sea, there have been Projects, true in theory but difficult to execute... One is by a Watch to keep time exactly. But because of the motion of the ship, the Variation of Heat and Cold, Wet and Dry, and the Difference of Gravity in different Latitudes, such a watch hath not yet been made.

Sir Isaac Newton.

Eventually a bill was put before Parliament 'for providing a public reward for such person or persons as shall discover the Longitude'. The Act offered rewards of up to twenty thousand pounds for a practical solution to the problem, a vast fortune in the money of the time.

The Marine Timekeeper

The easiest method for the navigator to determine his longitude is by comparing the time onboard ship with the time at a known point on the globe, for example Greenwich: the difference in time between the two points could readily be converted to degrees of longitude on a map. For example, if it is midnight on the ship and noon at Greenwich, the ship would be on exactly the opposite side of the globe – 180 degrees from Greenwich.

The theory was that a timekeeper on a ship would show the time at, say, Greenwich, while the navigator could fix local time by observing the angle of the sun or stars above the horizon. The difference between the two times showed how far east or west he was from Greenwich. In 1884, the prime meridian, the point from which longitude is measured, was internationally accepted as passing through the Royal Observatory, Greenwich. However, it took half a century to develop a portable timekeeper that would withstand the rigours of sea travel and keep time reliably to within a few seconds per day.

John Harrison, after a lifetime of single-minded endeavour, produced a series of marine timekeepers, which he submitted to the Board of Longitude. The first three were judged as worthy of encouragement, but not as offering a complete answer to the problem, and Harrison was awarded funds to further develop his ideas – an early example of government sponsorship in science. The first three timekeepers were large clocks using heavy, slow-moving balances as time controllers; Harrison eventually gave up on these and concentrated on developing the watch technology of the time for his final timekeeper, now known as H4.

Harrison realized that a smaller timepiece with fast-moving parts would be less subject to the motion at sea. He adapted many of his

earlier ideas together with new developments into H4, which, although highly complicated, performed brilliantly in the sea trial organized by the Board in 1762. The voyage to Jamaica took eighty-one days, and H4, accompanied by John Harrison's son William, lost just five

John Harrison. © *SCIENCE MUSEUM GROUP*

Harrison's H4 marine timekeeper. © *NATIONAL MARITIME MUSEUM*

seconds. This enabled him to calculate the ship's position, not within one degree of longitude as the Board stipulated for the award, but to an incredible 1.25 seconds, just one 2,880th part of one degree.

After another successful sea trial in 1764, Harrison believed that he had demonstrated that he had produced a timekeeper that would perform to the required accuracy. However, the Board of Longitude held back the final award of the prize until it could be shown that the device could be reproduced by other makers, ensuring that it would be of practical use. A long and bitter dispute dragged on for several years and the elderly Harrison was not noted for his diplomacy in dealing with the Board. However, he eventually agreed to disclose his secrets to a committee appointed by the Board, and to help with the construction of a copy of the timekeeper by an eminent London watchmaker, Larcum Kendall.

Kendall's copy of H4, known as K1, was taken by Captain Cook on his second great voyage of discovery in 1772 to the Pacific, and he reported that it had performed well. Kendall was asked by the Board to make a second copy of H4, but he declined because of the time it would take; however, he did make two more marine timekeepers of a simplified design, K2 and K3, but they failed to perform as well as the earlier watch. By then the relationship between Harrison and the Board had completely broken down, and it took the intervention of King George III, who had been persuaded to test H4

in his private observatory, to use his influence to have a bill put before Parliament that granted Harrison an award equivalent to the remainder of the £20,000 Longitude prize.

The reservations of the Board of Longitude were in fact well founded in that H4 was extremely complicated and was not suited to mass production. The whole point of the Longitude prize was to provide a practical solution to the longitude problem. The Board continued to offer rewards to any inventor who could come up with a more practical design; however, the conditions were so stringent that most of the horologists working on new designs eventually gave up applying for awards, although some funds were disbursed. Harrison's great achievement was to show that it was possible to solve the problems associated with making an accurate portable timepiece, and this gave the spur to the next generation of inventors to come up with a much simpler design.

All four of Harrison's marine timekeepers can now be seen at the National Maritime Museum in Greenwich. H5, a second watch made by Harrison, is owned by the Worshipful Company of Clockmakers and is on show in London's Science Museum.

The Problem of Temperature Error

Harrison's most important invention, which was taken up in future watch design, was his solution to the problem of temperature error. The timekeeping of a watch depends upon the

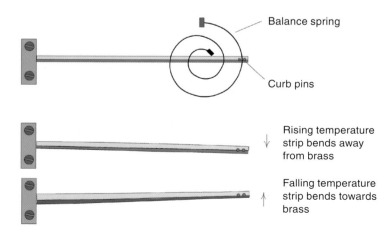

Balance spring

Curb pins

Rising temperature strip bends away from brass

Falling temperature strip bends towards brass

Harrison's compensation curb.

Le Roy marine timekeeper.

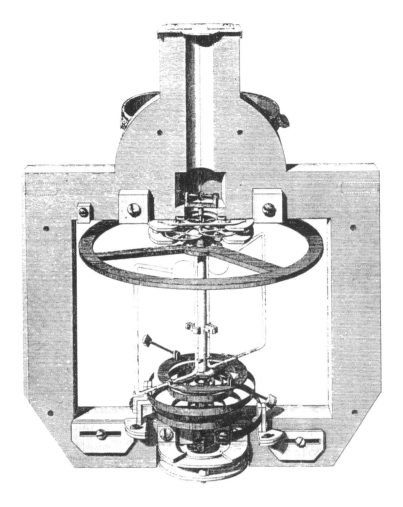

balance, which is controlled by the balance spring.
The problem with a spring
made from steel – or most
other metals – is that it loses
elasticity as the temperature
rises; this causes a losing rate
in rising temperatures and a
gaining rate as the temperature falls. Some means of
compensating for this change
had to be found, and Harrison came up with a brilliant
solution in a device that not
only revolutionized watch
design, but found a use in
later devices such as thermo-
stats. He used the difference
in the coefficient of expansion
of brass and steel to make an
automatic regulating device,
which became known as the
compensation curb.

Harrison's device consist-
ed of a strip of brass riveted to a strip of steel.
As the temperature rises, the brass expands
faster than the steel, causing the strip to bend
away from the brass section; the reverse hap-
pens in falling temperatures. The pair of curb
pins attached to the strip thus move along the
balance spring, shortening and lengthening its
effective length, thereby compensating for the
gaining and losing effects of changing temperatures.

THE PRACTICAL CHRONOMETER

The big breakthrough in the design of a reliable marine timekeeper that could be produced

at a reasonable price was the development of
a successful detached escapement. In all early
escapements the balance was in constant contact with the wheel train, and any kind of
friction affecting the free movement of the
balance will interfere with its naturally good
timekeeping qualities. The first detached
escapement was invented by Pierre Le Roy
(1717–1785) in Paris. He produced a series of
experimental marine timekeepers in the 1760s
with varying success, but despite encouraging results he seems to have lost interest in
this branch of horology. The real development of the chronometer was due to two
English makers: John Arnold and Thomas Earnshaw.

JOHN ARNOLD AND THOMAS EARNSHAW

John Arnold

John Arnold (1736–1799) was perhaps one of the most talented horological craftsmen of his age, as well as being a successful business-man. He achieved considerable fame in 1764 by presenting George III with an incredible repeat-ing watch set into a finger ring; at about 13mm diameter, it was a truly remarkable feat and one of the wonders of the age. Arnold received the sum of 500 guineas as a reward and refused an offer of double this from Catherine the Great of Russia to make a similar watch, giving as his reason that he wanted King George's watch to remain unique. Soon after this, he started seri-ous work on a series of marine timepieces using a form of detent escapement and an improved temperature compensated balance.

John Arnold.

Thomas Earnshaw.

Thomas Earnshaw

Thomas Earnshaw (1749–1839) did not have the resources that Arnold had at his disposal: his early life was a constant struggle to pro-vide for a large family, and he was forced to work for other more successful watchmakers. He did, however, find time to experiment with an improved form of detent escapement and balance wheel, which eventually became the standard form used in English chronometers. Earnshaw and Arnold remained bitter rivals, although both received some financial sup-port from the Board of Longitude. Each had his supporters as to who should claim precedence for the vital improvements that made the produc-tion of marine chronometers a practical proposi-tion.

The Earnshaw Spring Detent Escapement

The Earnshaw spring detent escapement was the most successful chronometer escapement and was used in almost all marine chronometers and many smaller pocket chronometers. The escape wheel has no contact with the balance wheel apart from when giving it an impulse every alternate swing; it also needs no lubrication. In the days when natural oils tended to thicken and dry up quickly, this was a great advantage. (To help understand the action of the escapement, find one of the many online animations.) The only real drawback that discouraged the use of the escapement in pocket watches was the fact that the escapement was not self-starting – if the watch was allowed to stop, it needed to be shaken or twisted to get it started.

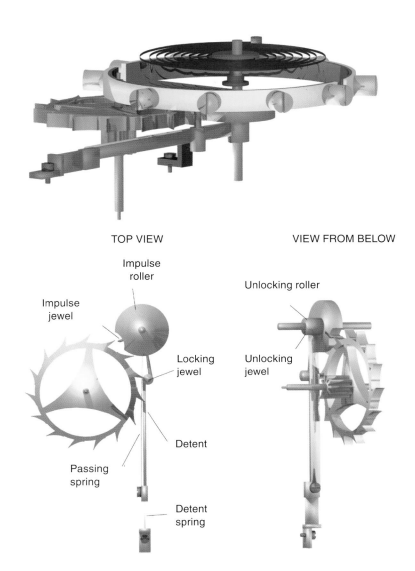

The Earnshaw spring detent escapement.

The Temperature-Compensated Balance

Using the principle of Harrison's compensation curb, both Arnold and Earnshaw (probably independently) designed balance wheels that used bi-metallic strips to form the rim of the balance wheel. As the temperature rises and the watch starts to lose, the rims bend inwards, causing a gaining rate, and vice versa as the temperature falls. Timing weights were attached to the balance arms, which could be adjusted to vary the amount of compensation (*see* later in the chapter).

Earnshaw's balance proved the more successful as he had developed a way of fusing the brass and steel elements of the wheel rim, rather than Arnold's method of riveting the brass and steel

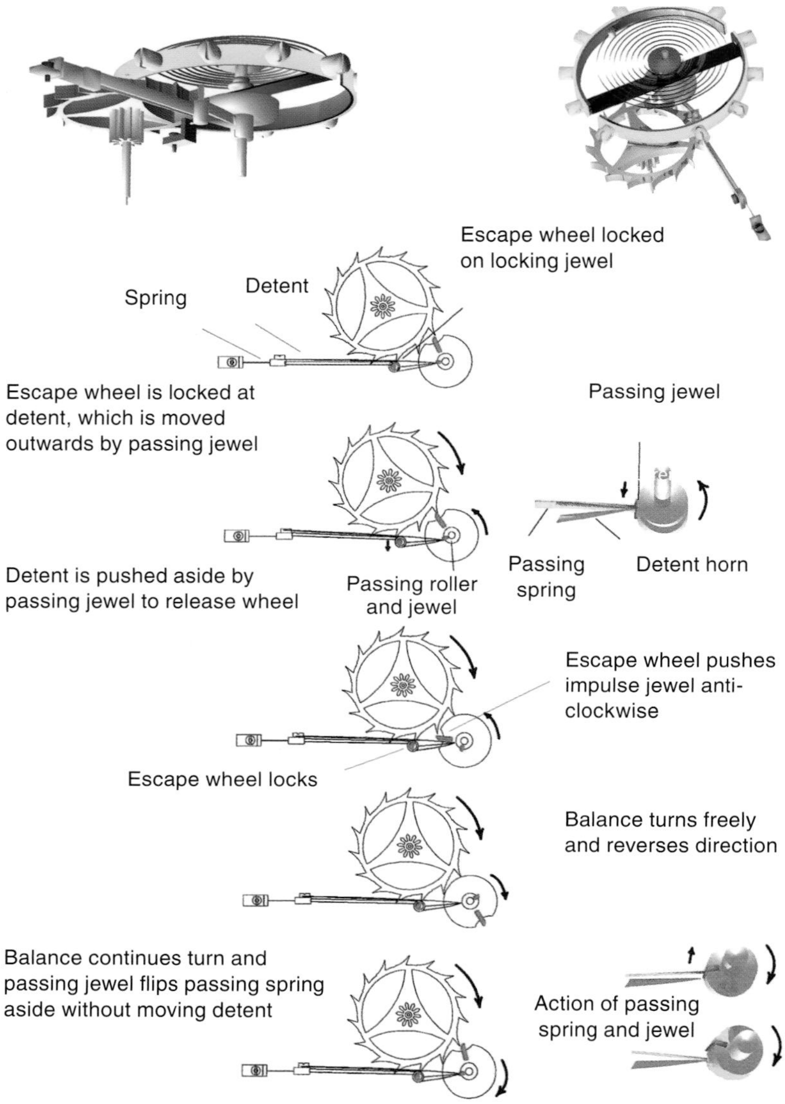

*The action of
the chronometer
escapement.*

Escape wheel locked
on locking jewel

Spring   Detent

Escape wheel is locked at
detent, which is moved
outwards by passing jewel

Passing jewel

Detent is pushed aside by
passing jewel to release wheel

Passing roller
and jewel

Passing   Detent horn
spring

Escape wheel pushes
impulse jewel anti-
clockwise

Escape wheel locks

Balance turns freely
and reverses direction

Balance continues turn and
passing jewel flips passing spring
aside without moving detent

Action of passing
spring and jewel

strips. This type of compensated balance was soon incorporated into precision watches and remained in use well into the twentieth century.

By the 1790s both Arnold and Earnshaw had set up factories for the production of marine and pocket chronometers. Soon, a large group of craftsmen began to specialize in the making of parts for chronometers. Many of the parts and rough movements were made in Prescot, Lancashire, by then the major centre of production of watch parts; the partly completed movements were then transported to London, where specialists in the Clerkenwell area finished the chronometers. For the next two centuries English makers supplied most of the world's shipping with affordable chronometers.

The incredible thing is that apart from some very minor improvements, the Earnshaw

The Earnshaw compensated balance.

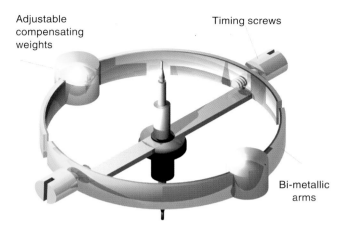

design was never changed, and instruments made in the late twentieth century were, in all important respects, identical to those produced in the late eighteenth century. Although the main market was marine chronometers for navigation, a limited number of pocket chronometers were produced throughout the nineteenth century and beyond, for customers demanding a precision of a second or two per day.

English makers generally used the Earnshaw pattern spring detent escapement, whilst continental makers preferred the pivoted detent type, which worked in exactly the same way although the detent was mounted on pivots instead of being supported by a spring.

It should be noted that although the term 'chronometer' was traditionally only applied to timepieces with a chronometer – that is, detent escapement – the Swiss watch industry began to use the term in the mid-twentieth century for some precision wrist watches. These were standard high quality lever watches that were specially regulated and submitted to an observatory for testing; they were granted a certificate confirming that they had performed within certain limits. Firms such as Rolex and Omega produced these watches in considerable numbers after World War II.

The Arnold pocket chronometer showing his compensated balance.

Typical late nineteenth-century Swiss pocket chronometer with pivoted detent escapement.

Chapter 6
Nineteenth- and Twentieth-Century Developments

THE EARLY LEVER ESCAPEMENT

Although high precision pocket chronometers were available from the late eighteenth century, they were not made in large numbers. The search went on for a reliable detached escapement that could be produced at a reasonable price. One of the leading London makers of the mid-eighteenth century, Thomas Mudge, began experimenting with a new escapement based on the successful anchor clock escapement. In 1770 he produced a watch with the new escapement, which George III presented to Queen Charlotte.

This escapement, with minor improvements, later known as the detached lever, became the most popular and successful of all watch escapements. It gave a sharp impulse on each swing and otherwise left the balance free to rotate; it was compact, reliable and relatively

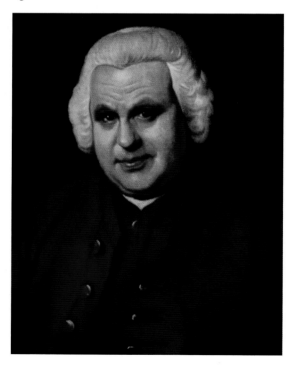

Thomas Mudge.

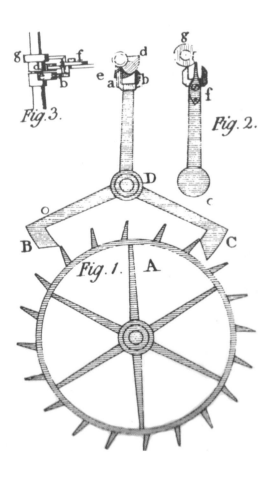

A contemporary drawing of the Mudge escapement.

The English lever escapement.

easy to manufacture, and unlike the chronometer escapement, it would start on its own when the watch was wound.

The escapement evolved into several forms: the English version used an escape wheel with slim ratchet teeth. This became the standard throughout England, and later in the nineteenth century it was produced in huge numbers by the Lancashire watch industry. These watches are generally known as English levers.

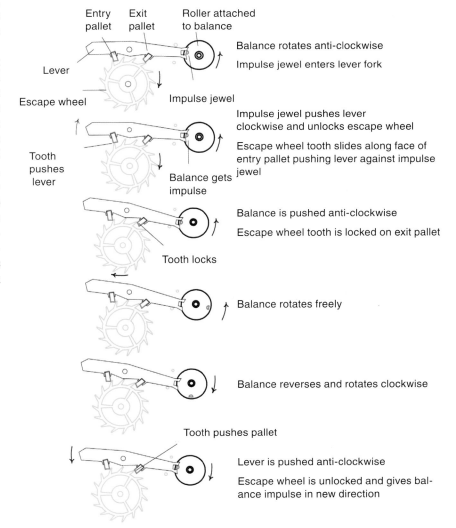

Entry pallet   Exit pallet   Roller attached to balance

Lever

Escape wheel

Impulse jewel

Balance rotates anti-clockwise

Impulse jewel enters lever fork

Impulse jewel pushes lever clockwise and unlocks escape wheel

Escape wheel tooth slides along face of entry pallet pushing lever against impulse jewel

Tooth pushes lever

Balance gets impulse

Balance is pushed anti-clockwise

Escape wheel tooth is locked on exit pallet

Tooth locks

Balance rotates freely

Balance reverses and rotates clockwise

Tooth pushes pallet

Lever is pushed anti-clockwise

Escape wheel is unlocked and gives balance impulse in new direction

The action of the lever escapement.

Typical English lever watch c.1880.

THE RACK-LEVER ESCAPEMENT

The rack-lever escapement was invented in 1792 by Peter Litherland (1756–1805), a Liverpool watchmaker. In many ways this was a retrograde step in escapement design, despite its popularity with Liverpool watchmakers in the early nineteenth century, perhaps because of its reliability. It replaces the lever fork and balance roller with a rack and pinion to drive the balance. However, the constant contact between the pallet rack with the pinion on the balance interfered with the free rotation of the balance, which was the big advantage of the original lever design.

Later in the nineteenth century, the American and Swiss industry adopted a more robust design with club-shaped teeth to the escape wheel. It is this design that is almost universally used in good quality modern watches.

An essential refinement to all types of lever escapement is the action of draw. In order to ensure safe locking of the lever against the banking pins, the two pallet stones are offset at a small angle (usually 10–15 degrees). This ensures that the movement of the lever continues after the impulse has been given. The lever is held firmly against each banking pin in turn so that in the event of a shock, it will stay in place and not interfere with the balance.

Rack-lever escapement.

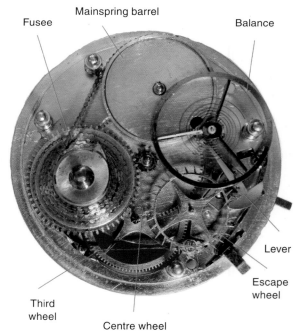

Rack-lever watch.

Despite its clear advantages, the lever escapement did not immediately replace the old verge escapement. Verge watches continued to be produced well into the nineteenth century, and cylinder escapements continued to be used in cheaper watches into the early twentieth century.

THE PIN-LEVER ESCAPEMENT

In 1867 George Frédéric Roskopf patented a new version of the lever escapement. His aim was to design a 'labourer's watch' that would sell for less than a week's wages earned by an unskilled worker. He dispensed with jewels and used stamped-out parts for most components; the escapement used steel pins set into the pallets rather than shaped jewels. Apart from this, the action of the escapement was exactly the same as the traditional lever version. His ideas were swiftly taken up by American companies such as Ingersoll and Waterbury in their 'dollar watches', and became the standard escapement for budget-priced watches until the 1970s, when cheap quartz watches were developed.

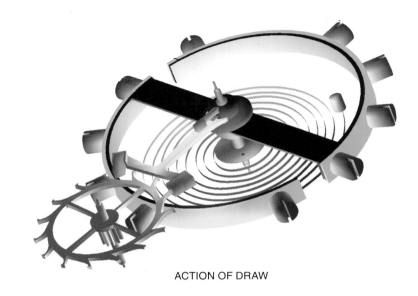

ACTION OF DRAW

Banking pin

Entry pallet

The lever is moving anti-clockwise and the corner of the entry pallet is locking on the wheel tooth.

Angle of draw

To draw the lever securely to the banking pin the entry pallet is slightly angled, the same with the exit pallet.

Club-toothed lever escapement.

The pin-lever escapement.

IMPROVEMENTS TO THE BALANCE SPRING

The first balance springs consisted simply of three or four coils of steel wire; later in the eighteenth century it was found that the per-

formance of the spring could be improved by increasing the number of coils, and experiments began with different shapes of spring. Arnold introduced the helical spring in his early chronometers, and with some small modifications, this became the standard form used in both marine and pocket chronometers.

The advantage of the helical spring was that, unlike the spiral spring, it did not pull the balance sideways as it expanded and contracted, and this lessened the friction on the balance pivots. The drawback was that this type of spring increased the thickness of the movement, which discouraged its use in watches. The material used was generally steel; however, Arnold often used gold for his springs, as it had the advantage of being resistant to rust. Many other materials were tried, particularly for marine chronometers, including glass. Later in the nineteenth century, a gold/palladium alloy was adopted by

Helical balance spring.

Typical nineteenth-century marine chronometer in box with gimbals.

several makers, including Thomas Mercer, the last English chronometer maker.

The great French horologist Breguet (1747–1823) improved the spiral balance spring by adding an overcoil – the outer coil of the spring was turned upwards and inwards, and this allowed the spring to wind and unwind more evenly. It was also found that altering the shape of the overcoil could affect the isochronism of the balance and improve positional errors. The best watches were generally described as adjusted in five or sometimes more positions – originally this meant that a highly skilled craftsman known as a 'springer' adjusted the shape of the overcoil to reduce the positional error of each watch. This was something of a black art, and springers worked as much by instinct and trial and error as by science.

New Alloys

In 1897, the Swiss physicist Charles Eduard Guillaume announced the development of a new iron/nickel alloy – invar. A sample of the material was sent to Paul Perret, a spring specialist who made a balance spring from it. To his surprise, he found that a watch fitted with the new spring showed a gaining rate with rising temperature – the reverse of a normal steel spring. He collaborated with Dr Guillaume in experimenting with nickel steel alloys to produce balance springs that showed very little change of elasticity with changes of temperature.

The first nickel/steel balance springs were introduced in 1899 under the name of Paul Perret spirals; the alloy later became known as elinvar. This eventually made the compensated balance redundant, and most watches from the mid-twentieth century used balance springs made from some form of this alloy with various additives. In recognition of the importance of his discovery, Dr Guillaume was awarded the Nobel Prize in 1920.

Antimagnetic Watches

Steel balance springs and those with alloys containing iron were prone to becoming magnetized, which caused the coils of the spring to

Early 20th-century compensated balance with overcoil balance spring

The Breguet overcoil balance spring.

Charles Éduard Guillaume.

stick together, resulting in a rapid gaining rate. The increasing sources of magnetism during the twentieth century made this a real problem; however, several new alloys were developed that had high resistance to magnetism and still maintained constant elasticity in changing temperatures.

DISPENSING WITH THE FUSEE

Whilst English makers remained attached to the traditional mainspring and fusee watch layout, some French and Swiss makers in the late eighteenth century abandoned the fusee altogether in what became known as the 'going barrel' design. The problem of varying power output of the mainspring when at the extremes of fully wound and almost run down was mitigated by using longer springs with a stop-work.

The Geneva Stop-Work

The Geneva stop-work was fitted to the barrel lid (*see* the diagram). The gearing limits the mainspring to four turns, and it is set up so that only the middle extent of the spring's run is used, avoiding the extremities of fully wound or run-down states.

In the diagram, A shows the mainspring wound to the maximum extent, with wheel 1 locked against the protruding tooth of wheel 2. B shows the spring starting to unwind, with wheel 1 turning wheel 2 one step at a time for five turns. In C the five turns are completed, and wheel 1 locks against wheel 2.

During the nineteenth century the going barrel design gradually replaced the fusee as it enabled simpler and slimmer watches to be made without significantly compromising accuracy. The advent of wrist watches in the twentieth century finally rendered the fusee obsolete.

SHOCKPROOF WATCHES

The delicate pivots of the balance were always prone to breakage when a watch was dropped, which necessitated making and fitting a new balance staff. This was quite a laborious process, which involved removing the balance spring and roller and using a set of 'turns' or a lathe to cut away the rivet holding the balance staff to the balance wheel — look again at the image on p.38, which shows a watchmaker using turns. The item to be worked on was held in the turns and rotated with a bow operated with one hand and whilst the other held a cutting tool called a graver to turn away metal.

Turning was an essential skill for a watchmaker, and traditional turns were used well into the twentieth century when small lathes made the job somewhat easier. However, using a lathe to turn a balance staff in no way improved the finished article, and a good watchmaker would be judged by the speed at which he could turn and fit a perfectly formed and polished staff.

A   Mainspring fully wound

Wheel 1

Wheel 2

B   Partly run down

C   After five turns mainspring locked

Geneva stop-work.

Shockproof jewelling.

Shock spring

Balance jewel

Breguet's parachute system *c*.1800

Shockproof Jewelling

The problem of break-age was first tackled by Breguet, with his para-cute suspension: the balance jewels were fixed to a spring that was designed to absorb a shock and return the balance to its proper position. During the twentieth century, particularly with the introduction of wrist watches, the idea was revived and a new form of jewelling for the balance assembly was developed. The older capped bearing was altered by fixing the jewel hole and endstone in a setting that fitted into the shock block in such a way that it would move up and down. A spring held the assembly in place (A in the image) until the balance received a shock (B), when the spring absorbed the energy allowing the shock setting to move upwards in the shock block – note that the balance staff is locked against the tube of the shock block. The assembly then returns to its original position.

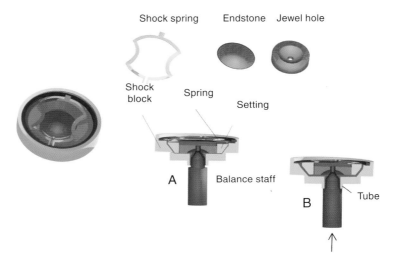

Incabloc anti-shock system

Shock spring   Endstone   Jewel hole

Shock block   Spring   Setting

A   Balance staff

B   Tube

The Incabloc device was one of the best-known systems introduced in the mid-1930s: it was used as a selling point, and 'Incabloc' was often printed on the watch dial.

Chapter 7
Complications

ALARM WATCHES

From the early days of the watch, alarm mechanisms were added, particularly to large watches. They were often known as clock watches or coach watches, and were often fitted with a pendant ring so they could be hung in a carriage.

REPEATING WATCHES

Portable striking clocks were developed in the mid-seventeenth century, and watches that struck the hours came soon after. The invention of the repeating mechanism, which allowed the owner to hear the time struck on a bell or gong in the back of the case by pressing a plunger, was claimed by both Edward Barlow and Daniel Quare; however, a patent was granted to Quare in 1689.

At first these watches simply struck the nearest hour; however, it wasn't long before quarter repeaters that used single strikes of the bell for the hour, then double strikes for each quarter hour, were developed. The ultimate repeating watch was the minute repeater, which used wire gongs sounding different notes to indi-

Repeating watch by Windmills, c.1695. The toothed rack on the upper side of the movement controls the number of hours struck.

French alarm watch c.1660.

Swiss skeletonized quarter repeater, c.1770.

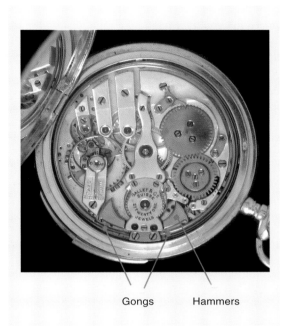

Gongs   Hammers

Minute repeating watch c.1900.

cate the time to the nearest minute; these appeared in the late eighteenth century.

However, the convenience of knowing the time in the dark came at a high price, as these watches were very expensive to produce. They have remained high-status possessions throughout the history of the mechanical watch, and in modern times, repeating mechanisms have been built into wrist watches.

Minute repeating under-dial work.

Quarter rack   Minute snail

Hour snail

Hour rack

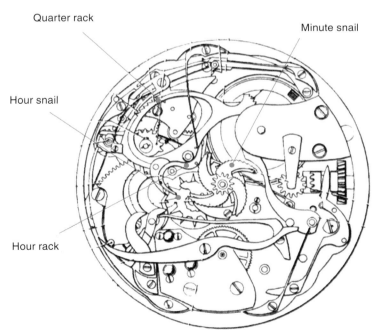

To sound the hour, the hour rack drops onto the hour snail, which turns with the hour hand. The twelve teeth on the upper part of the hour rack control the number of strikes of the gong. The quarters and minutes follow, controlled in the same way by their respective racks.

STOPWATCHES AND CHRONOGRAPHS

The term 'chronograph', literally meaning a time recorder, was originally applied to a watch designed to time an event: these would later be known as stopwatches. In more recent times, the term would be applied to watches with a timer built into the mechanism of a normal watch.

The French sculptor and horologist Louis Moinet (1768–1853) constructed his 'Compteur de Tierces' watch to aid the tracking of astronomical objects. This watch, rediscovered in 2013, has a centre seconds hand and three subsidiary dials to time intervals of up to twelve hours; it was also remarkable for its high-frequency balance, which beat at the unusually fast speed of thirty times per second, as compared

The Louis Moinet 'Compteur de Tierces' watch of 1816 (now preserved at the Ateliers Louis Moinet in St Blaise, Switzerland).

to the later standard of 5Hz. The watch is now preserved at the Ateliers Louis Moinet in St Blaise, Switzerland.

This watch pre-dated what was previously considered the first chronograph, developed by the French watchmaker Nicholas Mathieu Rieussec (1781–1866). Rieussec was commissioned in 1821 by Louis XVIII, a racing enthusiast, to make him a watch that could be used to time his horses. Although no longer regarded as the inventor, he was certainly the first maker to market this type of watch, to which he applied the name 'chronographe'.

Chronographs were rapidly taken up by the military to track artillery fire: by timing the interval between the firing of a shell and its explosion, the range could be simply computed. Watches with telemeter dials for instant calculation of distance compared to time, and tachymeters to calculate average speed (used by police forces to catch speeding drivers since the 1930s) were produced in large numbers.

Louis Moinet.

The Nicholas Rieussec 'chronographe' watch, 1845.

Telemeter dial.

LEFT: 1933 advert for the two-pusher chronograph.

BELOW: Breitling chronograph, 1915.

The first modern wrist chronograph with a thirty-minute counter was produced by Gaston Breitling in 1915; the Breitling firm went on to produce the first two-pusher model in the 1930s.

Chronograph Action

The push-pieces on the chronograph case operate a series of levers that start and stop the timer and return them to zero when the operation is finished. In 'A' in the figure (*see* page 60) the timer hands are driven by the centre chronograph wheel; this is caused to engage and disengage by the movement of the chronograph lever (coloured blue), which carries the intermediate wheel. This wheel rotates constantly, driven by the fourth chronograph wheel, which is attached to the fourth wheel of the main watch movement.

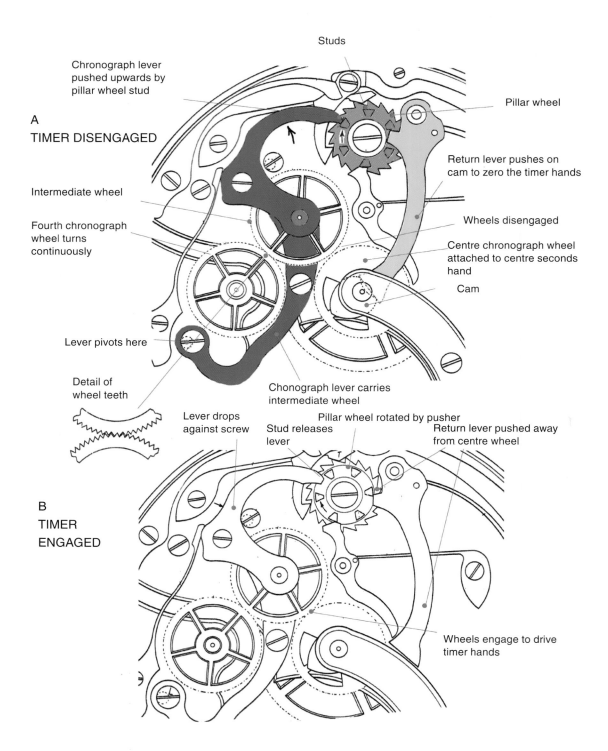

A
TIMER DISENGAGED

Studs

Chronograph lever
pushed upwards by
pillar wheel stud

Pillar wheel

Return lever pushes on
cam to zero the timer hands

Intermediate wheel

Wheels disengaged

Fourth chronograph
wheel turns
continuously

Centre chronograph wheel
attached to centre seconds
hand

Cam

Lever pivots here

Detail of
wheel teeth

Chonograph lever carries
intermediate wheel

Lever drops
against screw

Stud releases
lever

Pillar wheel rotated by pusher

Return lever pushed away
from centre wheel

B
TIMER
ENGAGED

Wheels engage to drive
timer hands

Chronograph action.

The pillar wheel (green) has six raised studs (red) and is rotated one step at a time by the depression of the push-piece.

As the pillar wheel moves round, the chronograph lever is lowered and raised by the studs to engage and disengage the centre wheel, starting and stopping the timer hands.

When the centre wheel is disengaged, the return lever (yellow) pushes the cam on the centre wheel to zero the timer hand.

In 'B' the timer is engaged, the centre wheel is being driven and the return lever is out of contact with the centre-wheel cam.

The Minute Recorder

Most chronographs have a subsidiary dial showing the minutes timed. In the first diagram 'A', the centre chronograph wheel (green) drives the intermediate wheel (blue) one tooth per

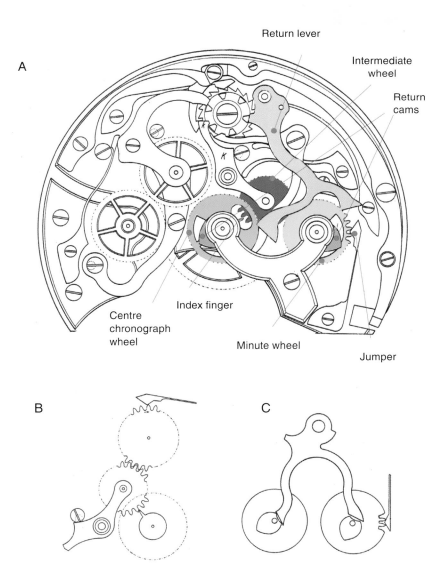

Minute recorder.

Gallet flying officer chronograph 1939.

Omega Speedmaster Professional worn by Neil Armstrong on the Apollo 11 mission – Smithsonian Institute.

revolution – that is, every minute – via the index finger. This is geared to the minute wheel (yellow), which is held in place by the jumper.

The next diagram 'B' shows the action in detail. The index finger is in the process of turning the intermediate wheel, which turns the minute wheel. The jumper is about to fall into the gap between the teeth, holding the wheel until the next minute.

The last diagram 'C' shows the return action. After the timer is stopped, the second pusher is depressed, which allows the return lever to drop between the column wheel studs and spring across to engage the two heart-shaped cams; these turn the two wheels to the zero position.

Thus the two timer hands are now reset at zero, ready for the next operation of the stopwatch.

The Gallet 'Flying officer' watch was commissioned by Senator Harry S. Truman in 1939 for navigators and pilots of the US Army Air Forces, and it was issued throughout World War II. It was the first watch to feature a rotating bezel and with time zones printed on the

The original Lemania/ Omega calibre 321 movement.

Buzz Aldrin wearing his Speedmaster on Apollo 11.

Rolex split-second chronograph, 1942.

Split-second chronograph movement.

worn outside a spacesuit on the moon. The watch had a movement made by Lemania, which was fitted with an Omega balance and Incabloc shockproofing. This was a great coup for Omega – probably the best piece of product placing in the history of advertising!

Split-Second Chronograph

The split-second chronograph has two independent centre seconds hands: the main seconds hand operates as normal, and the secondary hand can be started and stopped separately; for instance, two runners in a race can be timed with the same watch.

dial to keep track of local time as aircraft flew across lines of longitude; it was also the first chronograph to feature a water-resistant case.

The Omega Speedmaster, introduced in 1957, was a favourite watch with US test pilots, and due to its toughness, it was passed for use by the astronauts on the Apollo space missions – and survived the extraordinary rigours of being

AUTOMATIC WATCHES

The concept of self-winding watches probably originated with Abraham-Lois Perrelet (1729–1826), a Swiss watchmaker born in Neuchâtel. In the age of pocket watches, the winding energy came from an oscillating weight pivoted on

Early automatic movement with central rotor, signed Mazzi a Locarno c.1778.

A.L. Breguet 'Perpetuelle'.

Bust of A.L. Breguet at Père Lachaise cemetery.

one side of the movement; this moved up and down as the wearer walked.

Several makers in the late eighteenth century attempted to make a practical watch using this principle, notably the great French maker Abraham Louis Breguet who produced his first 'perpetuelle' in the 1780s. However, the concept proved unsatisfactory: no doubt the amount of energy stored during normal walking proved insufficient to keep the watch going for any useful length of time, and it ceased production in 1810.

The Rolls Automatic Watch

An early competitor in the race to produce an automatic wrist watch was Leon Hatot, a French watchmaker born in Châtillon-sur-Seine in 1883. In 1911 he set up business in Paris, and in the late 1920s began the development of an automatic watch without a rotor. His design used a rectangular case and a smaller watch movement that slid from side to side within the case on ball bearings. A ratchet system used this motion to wind the mainspring as the wearer moved his or her wrist. Hatot signed an agreement with Blancpain to produce the watches in 1930; they were marketed under the

JOHN HARWOOD (1893–1964)

John Harwood was born in Bolton, England. He served a watchmaking apprenticeship with Hirst Brothers of Oldham, then in 1922 moved to the Isle of Man where he set up in business. In 1923 he developed his first self-winding wrist watch and was granted a Swiss patent in 1924. His watch was based on a Swiss movement made by Anton Schild S.A., with a bolt-on unit consisting of a centrally mounted rotor with a simple ratchet system that wound in one direction only, geared to the mainspring. It had the distinction of having no winding button: the hands were set by a rotating bezel that was engaged by a sharp backward turn when a red indicator appeared on the dial, showing that the hands could be set.

In 1928 Harwood licensed Fortis to manufacture the watches in Switzerland, and Blancpain in France. Unfortunately the stockmarket crash and the following depression resulted in the failure of the Harwood Perpetual Watch Company in 1931.

The Harwood movement. Harwood automatic watch 1928.

The Harwood movement.

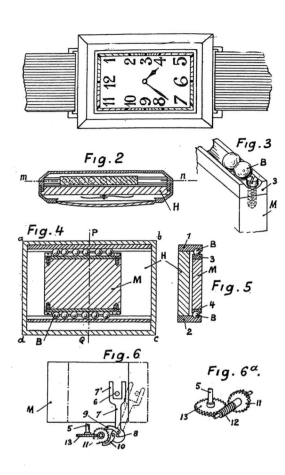

The Rolls automatic watch.

Patent drawings of the Rolls automatic watch.

name of 'Rolls' and were produced in different sizes for men and women. Production ceased in 1934.

The Rolex 'Perpetual'

Rolex patented their first automatic watch in 1931, the start of their highly successful 'Perpetual' range combined with their waterproof 'Oyster' case. The first models had a simple one-direction ratchet winding system with a self-contained automatic unit that screwed on to the main movement. The rotor rotated the full 360 degrees, and when fully wound, stored enough energy to keep the watch going for around thirty-five hours. This model proved very reliable and stayed in production for over twenty years.

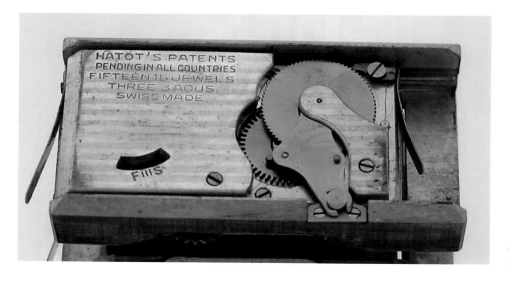

The Rolls sliding movement.

1931 Rolex perpetual.

First Rolex automatic movement 1931.

The Slipping Mainspring

One of the problems with early automatics was that when the mainspring was fully wound, a stopping device was needed to prevent continued winding as this could damage the winding wheels. The problem was solved by the development of the slipping mainspring. This involved redesigning the way the spring was attached to the inside of the spring barrel; instead of the usual hook that the mainspring latched on to,

the inner wall of the barrel was smooth. The mainspring had an extra length of spring riveted on its end, which wrapped round the outside of the coiled spring inside the barrel. The friction of this against the barrel wall allowed the spring to almost fully wind, and then the spring would start to slip, avoiding damage to the delicate wheels of the automatic work.

'Bumper' Automatic Movements

The Harwood automatic watches had an oscillating weight, which described an arc of about 240 degrees; at the end of each swing, the rotor hit a buffer spring, which helped the return swing. The wearer could feel a bumping action as the rotor operated. Unlike Rolex, with their 360-degree design, several important firms favoured the 'bumper' design, including Omega and Jaeger LeCoultre. The two designs are remarkably similar, using a rack-and-pinion

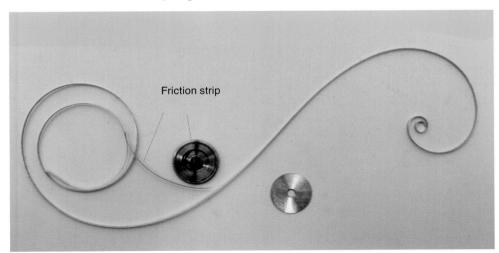

Friction strip

The slipping mainspring.

system to drive a ratchet wheel geared to the mainspring. These watches only wound in one direction; however, the design was robust and reliable.

The Omega Automatic

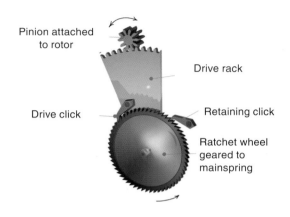

The Omega calibre 28.1 automatic.

The Omega calibre 28.1 was introduced in 1942 and featured rack-and-pinion winding with buffer springs for the rotor, together with Incabloc shock protection – *see* the image above. The rotor pinion is geared to the drive rack, which is given a reciprocating action by the swinging of the rotor. The drive click turns the ratchet wheel, which is geared to the mainspring, and a retaining click prevents the spring from unwinding. This model and its later ver-

sions, the 330 and 331 calibres, remained in production until the mid-1950s.

The Jaeger LeCoultre

The Jaeger LeCoultre calibre 476 was introduced in 1946, and the drive mechanism was very similar to the Omega 28.1. This watch also featured a reserve power indicator on the

The Jaeger LeCoultre automatic 1946.

Jaeger LeCoultre calibre 476 movement.

Jaeger LeCoultre Futurematic 1952.

Futurematic hand setting.

dial, which showed how many hours running were left – when red showed it was nearly run down; the feature involved an ingenious differential gear. In 1952 the company introduced the 'Futurematic' model: this had no winding crown, and the hands were set from the back of the watch.

shaped cam attached to the rotor. This delivered reciprocating motion to a rocking plate with a pair of clicks that drove a ratchet wheel geared to the mainspring. It was a delightfully simple device with few moving parts; it proved very successful and remained in production for over twenty years.

Two-Directional Winding

IWC (International Watch Company) was one of the first makers to introduce two-directional automatic winding and a rotor that turned through 360 degrees, thus making buffer springs redundant. In 1955 they launched their calibre 852, with a drive system that used a heart-

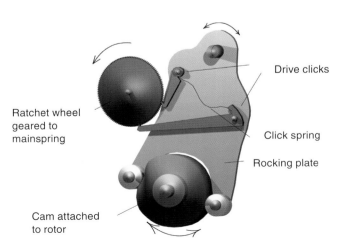

Drive clicks

Ratchet wheel geared to mainspring

Click spring

Rocking plate

Cam attached to rotor

IWC automatic system.

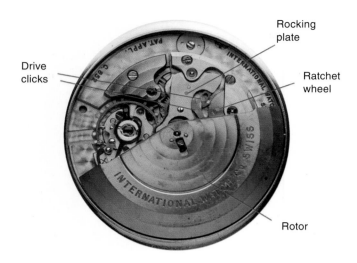

Drive clicks

Rocking plate

Ratchet wheel

Rotor

IWC calibre 852 movement.

gear (blue) is attached to the rotor, which is free to swing in both directions. Two intermediate wheels are mounted on pivoted arms (purple). The drive wheel (red) is geared to the mainspring. When the rotor turns anticlockwise, arm A is pulled away from the drive wheel, and the intermediate wheel B is pushed into contact with the drive wheel, turning it clockwise. When the rotor turns clockwise, lever A is pushed into contact with the drive wheel turning it clockwise, and wheel B moves aside. Thus whichever way the rotor turns, the drive wheel winds the mainspring.

CALENDAR MECHANISMS

Many of the earliest surviving clocks show dates and astronomical events, and it is not surprising that early watches also had date mechanisms. Surviving watches by Jean Vallier and other makers from the early seventeenth century have simple calendar works showing the date, day and month. However, these did not take into account the differing lengths of the month or leap years, and the date would have to be reset from time to time.

Other Automatic Systems

Many other automatic systems were developed in the 1950s and 1960s using various gear combinations. A simple and compact solution to winding through 360 degrees of rotor movement both ways, is illustrated in the accompanying diagram of automatic gearing. The rotor

Perpetual Calendars

In order to produce a watch that automatically corrects for months and leap years, a much more complicated mechanism is needed than the simple gearing of existing calendar works. Thomas Mudge, one of the most ingenious of all horological craftsmen, produced the first perpetual calendar watch in 1762; it is now in the British Museum collection. Other makers, including Breguet with his wonderful 'Marie Antoinette' watch (*see* Part II), made pocket watches with similar mechanisms. In the twentieth century sev-

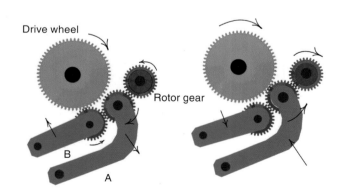

Drive wheel

Rotor gear

B

A

Automatic gearing.

eral manufacturers, including Patek Phillipe in 1925 and LeCoultre in 1937, produced wrist watches with perpetual calendars.

Many calendar watches show the age of the moon, the gearing usually giving a display of phases in a twenty-nine-and-a-half-day cycle. The average lunar cycle is actually twenty-nine days, twelve hours, forty-four minutes and 2.8 seconds. Converting the twelve-hour watch cycle to something like the true lunar cycle using as few gears as possible is an interesting mathematical problem. It is possible to get within a few seconds per cycle with just three gears, and watches have been made with several combinations of wheels and pinions.

The calendar work illustrated shows several features common to many versions. A wheel that rotates every four years controls the length of each month. A lever drops into a different slot each month, and the depth of the slot controls the number of days for that month – note the deeper slots for February and the slightly less deep slot that comes round every four years.

Jaeger LeCoultre perpetual calendar.

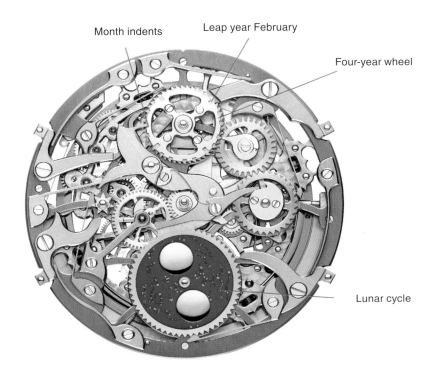

Perpetual calendar work.

Chapter 8
Efforts to Improve Timekeeping

LUBRICATION

Breguet was quoted as saying 'give me the perfect oil and I will give you the perfect watch'. Whilst this was, of course, an overstatement, it does illustrate the problems all horological craftsmen have had in obtaining suitable lubricants. Early oils were made from either animal or vegetable fats. Various sources included the sperm whale, fish oil, olive oil and neat's foot oil – derived from animal bones.

Attempts were made to purify these fatty oils, and in general they had good lubricating properties when freshly applied, but they tend to thicken over time and to change their qualities under the influence of changes in temperature and humidity. These changes had inevitable consequences on the timekeeping of watches, and the deterioration of oils would cause

wear on pivots and bearings, which would eventually stop the watch. The only remedy was to clean off old oil residue regularly, and to relubricate.

Some improvements were made to fatty oils by blending them with mineral oils and anticatalysts that improved their stability, but performance under severe conditions was still a problem. Early synthetic oils produced in the 1920s were found to be unsuitable for watch use, and the chemical industry was reluctant to develop special lubricants for the watch industry as the cost of development would have been prohibitive considering the small quantities required. It required the watch industry to fund research and development, which began in 1939 in the USA, Switzerland and Germany.

By the 1950s several new synthetic oils were becoming available that were a great improvement on earlier natural oils, offering greater stability and resistance to spreading and evaporation.

MICROMETER REGULATORS AND BEAT SETTING

Regulating a watch to within a few seconds per day with a traditional simple regulator could be a frustrating and time-consuming process, particularly when it had to be done by checking against a master clock each day. Moving the regulator a very small amount was difficult, and more precise devices were developed with some kind of adjusting screw to make very small movements easier to control. The most popular was the 'swan neck' regulator introduced in the mid-nineteenth century, which is still often used in precision watches.

Regulator

Adjusting screw

Balance spring stud

Beat adjuster

Swan-neck regulator and beat adjuster.

Beat Setting

In addition to regulating the watch, it is important that it is set precisely 'on beat' – that is, with the impulse being given at the centre of the arc made by the balance. This had to be done by observing the balance at rest, and ensuring that the impulse jewel was resting in the centre of the pallet fork. Adjusting this was a laborious process that involved removing the balance and turning the balance spring on the balance staff.

With the development of electronic timing machines in the mid-twentieth century watch timing was revolutionized: machines such as the vibrograph compared the rate of the watch with an accurate quartz time base, and also gave a printout of the beat setting; in addition, later machines gave a readout of the balance amplitude. Most makers abandoned the fixed-balance spring terminal and replaced it with an adjustable arm that allowed for easy adjustment of the beat setting.

HIGH-FREQUENCY BALANCES

Another way to improve accuracy, which Harrison used in his final H4 timepiece, was to make the balance lighter and increase the frequency of the oscillations. Up until the mid-twentieth century, most watches worked at 18,000 'vibrations' (an old term for 'oscillations') per hour, or 5Hz. Later, makers increased this to 19,800 or 21,600, and some went further, with higher frequencies up to 36,000 – although this had the disadvantage of using more power, which necessitated making the components smaller – and of course wear on components was bound to increase.

Making higher frequency watches does not necessitate increased manufacturing costs, so some makers opted for the higher frequencies to improve the time-keeping of modestly priced watches, whilst others concentrated on more traditional means of improving timekeeping. With the introduction of lighter, faster-moving balances, it was found that the overcoil form of spring could be abandoned without significantly affecting timekeeping, and most makers adopted the simple flat balance spring, which had the added attraction of reducing the thickness of the movement.

THE FREE-SPRUNG BALANCE

Some makers took up the type of balance used by marine chronometer makers and dispensed with the regulator that shortened or lengthened the effective length of the balance spring. These 'free-sprung' balances, as we have seen, were regulated by adjusting timing screws around the rim of the balance. This was fine in the large marine chronometer mechanisms, but producing small free-sprung watch balances and developing methods of adjustment was costly and became a feature of high-quality movements.

In the 1970s Rolex adopted a free-sprung balance with tiny gold adjusting screws with

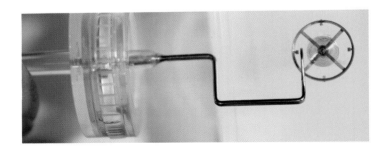

Rolex free-sprung balance and adjuster.

star-shaped heads. These screws can be moved very precisely with a special tool that allows screws on the opposite side of the balance to be turned by the same amount so as not to upset the poising of the balance. The pairs of screws are turned inwards to make the watch gain and outwards to lose. Other makers such as Vacheron & Constantin and Patek Phillipe used similar balances.

POSITIONAL ERROR

Gravity has a small effect on the rate of even the best watches. A watch timed in one position – say, dial up – would show a slightly different rate to dial down or other positions. As we have seen, watchmakers went to great lengths to poise their balance wheels – that is, making sure that the rim of the wheel and its associated timing weights were equally balanced so that turning it to different positions had as little effect as possible.

However, the changing friction of the balance pivots in their bearings was still a problem. This was mitigated by using special jewels with the inner surface of the holes curved to reduce the contact with the balance staff pivots. The object was to equalize the surface contact of the pivot when upright, resting on the endstone, and sideways when the pivot rubs against the side walls of the jewel hole.

The effect of gravity on the delicate coils of the balance spring would make a tiny difference to the rate; altering the shape of the terminal curves – the curves at the extreme ends of the spring – could improve positional error. Thus it became common from the late nineteenth century to describe a high-quality watch as 'timed in five positions' or even more, originally indicating that it had been individually adjusted to average out the variations in several different positions.

The highly skilled craftsmen who adjusted the springs were known as 'springers', and their work was as much an art as a science, relying on instinct and experience. Modern 'chronometer' watches are still generally described as 'adjusted to five positions and temperature', although individual adjustment is rarely done.

THE TOURBILLON

In an attempt to equalize the changing positions whilst a watch is worn, Breguet patented a device that he named the 'tourbillon' (from the French for 'whirlwind') in 1801, which he had developed around 1795. He mounted the escapement – that is, the balance, pallets and escape wheel of the lever escapement – in a carriage that rotated on a horizontal plane, normally once per minute.

This was a great triumph of watchmaking and a beautiful thing to behold; however, it is arguable as to whether or not it contributed greatly to the accuracy of the watch. A perfectly poised balance is hardly at all affected by position changes – far more important are changes in lubrication and variations of power from the mainspring.

Bahne Bonniksen (1859–1935), who worked in Coventry, England, produced a simplified slower moving version that he named the 'Karrusel'. He produced a series of fine watches, one of which in 1903 came first in the deck watch

Breguet tourbillon watch.

Modern tourbillon carriage.

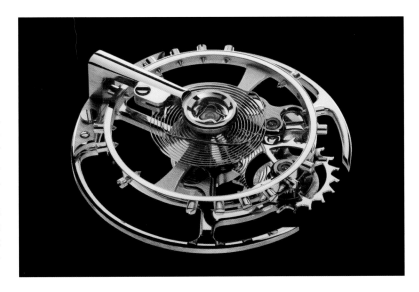

trial at the Royal Greenwich Observatory; it was purchased by the Admiralty for the then considerable sum of £22, and can now be seen at the Maritime Museum, Greenwich. The tourbillon has enjoyed a comeback as a feature in high-value wrist watches, as an ultimate example of the watchmaker's art.

Detail of a modern tourbillon watch by Laurent Ferrier.

PART II:

WATCHMAKING IN FRANCE

Breguet watch.

Chapter 9
The Beginnings in France

There is some doubt as to the location of the first centre of watch production; the earliest surviving watches come from South Germany, but it is possible that French clockmakers in Blois were working along the same lines in the late fifteenth century. The earliest record of watch manufacturing in France is an order from King François I in 1518:

> …[to] pay to Julien Coudray clockmaker at Blois the sum of 200 gold écus: as payment for two fine daggers, their hilts containing two gilt orloges destined for the King's service.

We first need to question whether the term 'orloge' refers to a watch or a sundial. The claim that these are the earliest recorded French watches, rather than small sundials, is supported by the fact that Coudray was a well-known clockmaker. Also, examples of watches set in sword and dagger hilts do survive, albeit from some ninety years later; no sword hilts with sundials are known. Further evidence of French watch production in the early sixteenth century comes from the 1532 will of a royal treasurer, Florimond Robertet. He left twelve watches, one of which '… shows all the stars and the celestial signs and motions'; it is also

The Château de Chambord near Blois.

notable for the earliest known use of the word *montres* rather than the earlier *orloges*.

G. H. Baillie (*Watches, Their History and Development*) points out that evidence based on the accounts of a single maker (Peter Henlein)...

... is not sufficient [evidence] to prove the accepted view that the watch industry started in Nuremberg. There is, too, an essential difference between the mechanisms of the German and French watches, which is evidence that the French did not copy from the Germans but made an independent start.

WATCHMAKING IN BLOIS

Blois seems to have been the first important centre of French watchmaking. This area of the Loire valley was something of a playground for the French court, which built magnificent hunting lodges such as the Château de Chambord, begun by François I in 1519, just down the road from Blois. With an abundance of wealthy and fashion-conscious clients on their doorstep it is hardly surprising that Blois became a centre of excellence in decorative crafts.

The earliest known surviving French watch, dated 1551, is by Jacques de la Garde of Blois, a watchmaker to the king from 1578 to 1580. Sur-

viving examples of French watches made before 1590 are extremely rare, although watchmakers are recorded in Autun, Rouen, Lyons, Sedan, Angoulême, Loches, Dijon and Grenoble as well as Paris. A notable Lyons watchmaker, Jean Vallier, is recorded as working in 1596 until his death in 1649; several fine watches have survived from this maker.

Watch by Jacques de la Garde, Blois — 1551.

Watch by Jean Vallier with champlevé enamel c.1630.

ENAMELLING

Watch by Nicholas Bernard, Paris, with case by Suzanne de Court. Early seventeenth century.

The early seventeenth-century watch shown is by Nicholas Bernard, Paris; it has an enamel case by Suzanne de Court, who was active in Limoges in the late sixteenth and early seventeenth centuries, although her birthdate is unknown. Scholars believe she may have been the daughter of the enameller Jean Court, and she is the only female enameller known to have been working in Limoges in that period. The image (right) shows a watch case also enamelled in Limoges by Jean Reymond, with very similar scenes, taken from woodcuts by Bernard Saloman that portray Apollo and Daphne. This case was imported into London and fitted with a movement by David Ramsay, the Scottish-born clockmaker to James I of England, *c.*1620.

Watch c.1620 with Limoges case and English movement by David Ramsay.

A new enamelling technique pioneered in Blois has been credited to Jean Toutin (1578–1644); this involved applying opaque colours to a white enamel ground, producing an effect closely resembling a miniature painting. The cost of producing watch cases with this type of enamelling was enormous. Each colour had to be separately fired at a very precise temperature to avoid damage to earlier layers, and the failure rate was high. Only the patronage of the wealthiest court in Europe could have made this exquisite work possible, and it has never been matched.

Watch by Nicholas Gribelin, Blois, c.1650.

These enamellers were clearly well aware of the latest artistic trends and often produced copies of recent paintings. The watch shown here is by Nicholas Gribelin, a member of a family of makers active in Blois and Paris from the late sixteenth century. The enamelled case front is copied from a painting of Anthony and Cleopatra by Sebastian Bourdin.

One of the most important watches of the period, now in the Metropolitan Museum of Arts in New York, is by Jacques Goullons (active in Paris, 1626 – he died in 1671). It dates from 1645–48 and depicts the young Louis XIV on horseback, with the arms of Navarre on the back.

THE FRENCH WARS OF RELIGION

It has been estimated that over half of French watchmakers were Protestants, particularly Huguenots, who held to the Reformed or Calvinist tradition. The Huguenot community by the mid-sixteenth century made up about 10 per cent of the population. This generally sober, well educated and industrious group prospered, and tensions with the Catholic population grew. The result was a series of religious conflicts known as the 'French Wars of Religion', which were

Watch by Jacques Goullons, Paris, 1645–48, depicting Louis XIV.

St Bartholomew's Day massacre — Françoise Dubois.

fought intermittently between 1562 and 1598. One of the worst atrocities has become known as the 'St Bartholomew's Day Massacre', which began in Paris on 24 August 1572 and spread to the provinces over the next months. Thousands of Huguenots were killed by Catholics, around 25,000 in Paris alone and up to 70,000 in all.

Many Huguenots looked for refuge in other Protestant countries, and the Huguenot population in France, estimated at two million in 1572, had declined to less than one million by 1700. England and Switzerland in particular benefited from the influx of a talented and industrious workforce, and the watchmaking industries of both countries benefited at the expense of the French.

The loss of so much talent, particularly to London and Geneva, contributed to the French watchmaking industry losing the early lead it had during the sixteenth century. During the seventeenth century London makers outclassed the French in terms of quality of workmanship and technical innovation, and the Geneva makers, with their superior organization and entrepreneurial talent, undercut the high prices of French products.

Chapter 10
Eighteenth-Century Progress

Shortly after Charles II established the Royal Society in England, Louis XIV, at the suggestion of Jean-Baptiste Colbert, founded the French Académie des Sciences in 1666, to encourage and protect the spirit of French scientific research. In 1699 the King installed the company in the Louvres with a set of rules and the title Royal Academy of Sciences; he also established a yearly publication with descriptions of work done by its members. One of the first important scientific voyages sponsored by the Academy was in 1672–3, when Jean Richer was sent to Cayenne (Guiana) to establish at that latitude the length of a seconds-beating pendulum. Richter found that the pendulum measured 990mm at that site, compared with 994 in Paris. Huygens, using Newton's new law of gravitation, deduced from this that the Earth was not a perfect sphere, but was wider at the equator and flattened at the poles.

Despite Newton's agreement, many French astronomers refused to accept the theory, and it took two further expeditions to confirm the Huygens/Newton hypothesis. This interest in the latest scientific ideas and development of new instruments was not just confined to the Académie, but was taken up by fashionable society, and the latest discoveries were common subjects for discussions in the Paris salons.

Given this positive interest in scientific matters it is not surprising that the longitude problem (see Part I) was as high on the agenda in France as it was in England. The importance of accurate navigation was as vital to the French with their growing empire as it was to the British. David S. Landes (*Revolution in Time*) writes:

> The search for the longitude was perceived from the beginning as a project of intellectual and humanitarian concern transcending national interests and boundaries. This is

not to say that the spirit of competition was absent. On the contrary the participating scientists and mechanics were as sensitive as ever to questions of priority, while their rulers and countrymen drew honour from their achievements.

It is perhaps surprising that at a time of intense rivalry and endless wars over colonial possessions and trade, the results of expensive expeditions and investigations were widely disseminated in the scientific community, rather than kept close as state secrets. The English Board of Longitude, for example, insisted that any successful solution to the problem of finding longitude must be fully explained and published. The Paris Observatory, founded in 1667, which pre-dated the Greenwich Observatory, published the world's first national almanac, the *Connaissance des temps*, in 1679, using eclipses of Jupiter's satellites to aid seafarers in establishing longitude.

PIERRE LE ROY'S SEA CLOCK

One of the most important developments in the long quest to build a successful 'sea clock' capable of keeping accurate time on an ocean voyage, was made by Pierre Le Roy, the leading French horologist of his generation. Born in 1717 in Paris, the son of Julien Le Roy, clockmaker to Louis XV, he produced a marine clock in 1766 that was a radical departure from John Harrison's H4 timepiece, which had been completed two years earlier (see Part I). Instead of concentrating on improving existing watch technology, as Harrison had done, he started from fundamental principles by designing a revolutionary form of detached escapement that allowed the balance wheel of his clock to rotate freely, except when it received its impulse.

Le Roy's sea clock was entered for tests for the prize offered by the Académie. These were initially encouraging; however, the clock was extremely delicate and proved unreliable on prolonged sea trials. Despite several attempts to improve his design, Le Roy eventually abandoned the project. It was left to two Englishmen in the mid-1770s, John Arnold and Thomas Earnshaw, to perfect the detached escapement pioneered by Le Roy and make the first successful marine chronometers. There is no indication that either Arnold or Earnshaw was familiar with the French escapement design, and it is not clear who deserves credit for the invention – but although Earnshaw's design proved the most successful, Le Roy was certainly first in the field.

Pierre Le Roy's sea clock, 1766.

The result of these efforts was that French makers lost the initiative, and this allowed their English counterparts to dominate the chronometer industry. Le Roy, in a letter written in 1783, shortly before his death, commentated on the inertia of French makers:

> This is the more unfortunate in that the reputation of our watch and clock industry abroad may be affected by it. If England alone is engaged in manufacturing marine chronometers, if we have nothing to oppose to theirs, other countries will conclude that the English are better than we in all horological work.

JEAN-ANTOINE LEPINE

Lepine (1720–1814) was apprenticed in Paris to André-Charles Caron, the clockmaker to Louis XV. He eventually married Caron's daughter and set up business with his father-

Jean-Antoine Lepine.

FERDINAND BERTHOUD, FOUNDER OF THE FRENCH MARINE CHRONOMETER INDUSTRY

Born in Switzerland in 1727, Berthoud came from a distinguished Neuchâtel family of clockmakers; at the start of his career he was apprenticed to his brother Jean-Henry in 1741. At the age of eighteen he moved to Paris to continue his studies, and it has been suggested that he was employed for a while by Julien Le Roy. He was clearly an impressive young man who, at the age of twenty-six, was already enjoying royal patronage; in 1753 the King ordered that he should be granted the official title of Master Watchmaker, in an exception to the guild rules of the time.

Berthoud was entrusted by Diderot to contribute a number of articles on watchmaking for his great *Encyclopédie méthodique*, and he continued publishing works on horological subjects throughout his life. He had a particular interest in sea clocks, and in 1763 was appointed by the King to join a group from the French Académie

ABOVE: Ferdinand Berthoud.

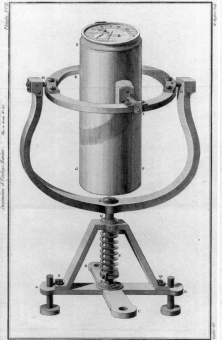

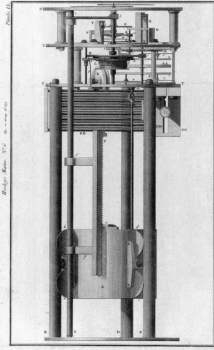

Drawings for Berthoud's sea clock no. 6, 1768.

to inspect Harrison's sea clocks in London. However, the party was refused permission to examine H4, the most advanced of Harrison's timepieces. During the 1760s Berthoud produced a number of sea clocks financed by the French Navy, experimenting with different forms of escapement and temperature compensation.

By the 1770s he had adopted a design that shows strongly the influence of Le Roy's work, and by the 1780s he was producing chronometers along the same lines as Arnold and Earnshaw in England. By the time of his death in 1807 he had produced over seventy marine chronometers, and can be regarded as the founder of the French marine chronometer industry. His nephew Louis continued his chronometer business; he was awarded a pension of 10,000 francs by Bonaparte on condition that he train five apprentices in the art of chronometer making.

Berthoud marine chronometer, 1780s.

in-law in 1765. Caron, meanwhile, abandoned watchmaking and assumed the title of Caron de Beaumarchais. He became better known as a businessman and playwright, attaining immortality as Mozart's librettist. Lepine is principally renowned for the invention of a new design of watch, which was taken up by Breguet and later by the Swiss industry.

George Washington, after he retired as President, was clearly up with the latest trends, as his letter of 1788 to Gouverneur Morris in Paris shows:

> Dear Sir,
> I had the pleasure to receive by the last mail your letter dated the 12th of this month. I am much obliged by your offer of executing commissions for me in Europe, and shall take the liberty of charging you with one only. I wish to have a good gold watch procured for my own use; not a small, trifling, nor finically ornamented one, but a watch well executed in point of workmanship, and of about the size and kind of that which was procured by Mr. [Thomas] Jefferson for Mr. [James] Madison, which was large and flat. I imagine Mr. Jefferson can give you the best advice on the subject, as I am told this species of watches, which I have described, can be found cheaper and better fabricated in Paris than in London…

Washington sent Morris a bank draft for twenty-five guineas, and after making some enquiries and rejecting several makers, Morris wrote back three months later:

> …I found at last that Mr L'Epine is at the head of his profession here, and in consequence asks more for his work than any body else. I therefore waited on Mr L'Epine and agreed with him for two watches exactly alike, one of which for you and the other for me…

Lepine's 'Going Barrel' Design

For his new calibre, Lepine dispensed with the traditional fusee and chain, using a simple spring barrel incorporating the great wheel; this became known as a 'going barrel' design. He adopted the new cylinder escapement (*see*

Lepine calibre watch c.1800.

Frédéric Japy.

Part I), which replaced the old verge with its bulky contrate wheel. Thus, every wheel was now parallel to the bottom plate, and each wheel had a separate bridge. The balance was no longer placed above the top plate but on the same plane as the rest of the wheels. The thickness of the movement now depended only on the size of the spring barrel, and with the new style, open-faced design of case, the entire watch was a fraction of the thickness of the traditional verge watch.

FRÉDÉRIC JAPY AND FACTORY PRODUCTION

Frédéric Japy was a pioneer in developing watch factories in both France and Switzerland. From a wealthy family in Beaucourt, then an enclave of the Duchy of Württemberg on the French side of the Jura, Japy set up in business as a watchmaker in 1771. His workshop in Beaucourt supplied rough movements and parts for the Swiss watchmakers of Neuchâtel across the border. His business prospered, and in 1776 he raised the significant sum of 600 *Louis d'or* to acquire a number of machines, commissioned to his own design from the Swiss firm of Jenneret-Gris of Le Locle. Within a few years his new power-driven factory was producing over 100 standard verge movements (*ébauches*)

per day at a cost of two and a half francs each, undercutting the Swiss ébauche makers. They were mostly supplied to the finishing trade of the Jura, who within ten years were importing around 100,000 per annum.

In order for the Swiss to avoid relying on French ébauches, a factory on the same lines was set up in Fontainemelon by the Benguerel and Humbert families. By 1797 the company employed 120 workers, and by 1841 the factory — Fabrique d'Horlogerie de Fontainemelon (FHF) — was supplying most of the movements used by the watchmakers in the cantons of Neuchâtel and Berne. Meanwhile Japy diversified production, and his firm began mass producing not only clocks, but all kinds of domestic appliances and office equipment well into the twentieth century.

THE INFLUENCE OF ABRAHAM-LOUIS BREGUET

Born, like Berthoud, in the Prussian principality of Neuchâtel in 1747, Breguet also made his career in France, becoming not only the principal horologist of his day, but along with John Arnold, one of the greatest watchmakers of all time. The Breguet family were Huguenots who sought refuge in Switzerland after the Revocation of the Treaty of Nantes (1685), which removed protection from French Protestants. Abraham-Louis' father died when he was eleven, and his mother then married Joseph Tattet, a watchmaker who had a showroom in Paris. At fifteen Abraham-Louis was sent to Paris and was apprenticed to an unidentified watchmaker at the Royal Court of Versailles; he also studied mathematics at evening classes run by the Collège Mazarin, part of the University of Paris.

Through the college, Abraham-Louis came to the attention of the Abbé Marie, who was the tutor to the children of the Comte d'Artois: he took an interest in the young man, and brought his talents to the notice of the king. Such powerful contacts were all-important to an ambitious artisan in a business that relied on aristocratic patronage, and set the young Breguet off to a good start on what was to become a glittering career path. A setback came with the deaths of both his mother and stepfather, which left Breguet to support himself and his younger sister.

Little is known about the period between him finishing his apprenticeship around 1767 and his marriage in 1775, when he set up in business at the Quay d'Horloge. It is possible that he worked at some time for Ferdinand Berthoud: a clock, signed 'Breguet No. 11', has survived, which is identical to those produced in Berthoud's workshop; also, a later chronometer watch (No. 12, dated 1809) is described by George Daniels in *The Art of Breguet* as '… made wholly to the design of Berthoud … It is possible … that it was brought forward by Breguet from an earlier period, and if this is so it would add weight to the story that Breguet worked for Berthoud before starting his own business.'

It is also probable that Breguet visited London in the period before his marriage, as some of his surviving watches made between 1775 and 1787 have English jewelling, and one has an English minute repeating mechanism. Breguet certainly had a strong friendship with John Arnold, then the most famous watchmaker in Europe – indeed, Arnold was later to send his son John Roger to work under Breguet in Paris, and Breguet likewise sent his son Louis to Arnold in London.

A.L. Breguet.

The 'Perpetuelle'

Breguet was by nature an inventor, and took no pleasure in the routine production of everyday watches. His ambition lay in designing complex and innovative timepieces for the wealthy aristocracy of Europe. One of his earlier enthusiasms was the perfection of the self-winding mechanism, which had been invented by the Swiss watchmaker Abraham-Louis Perrelet (1729–1826). Perrelet produced a number of pocket watches with a sprung weight, the movement of which was intended to wind the watch whilst the wearer was walking. Breguet was taking a considerable risk in investing a great deal of his business capital in the venture. He subsidized his experiments by selling ordinary watches and simple repeaters, the basic movements of which were supplied by Swiss ébauche makers, and finished at the Breguet workshop in Paris.

By 1786 Breguet was satisfied that his self-winding watch, which he named the 'Perpetuelle', was ready for quantity production. To raise the necessary finance he formed a partnership with the watch merchant Xavier Gide in 1787. However, sales were poor, and many watches were left unfinished, as Breguet spent much of his time away from the workshop taking orders for watches and clocks. He visited England on three occasions, in 1787, 1790 and

Breguet early 'Perpetuelle', 1782.

1791, doing business with the Royal Court and various members of the aristocracy.

Gide complained that Breguet could not resist making changes to customers' orders: in 1791 he wrote to Breguet: 'the trouble with your methods is that you do not make two watches alike. You have grand ideas but they must be put into practice.' Later that year the partnership was dissolved, and Breguet purchased the remaining stock of the business.

Switzerland

Trade improved, and by 1793 Breguet had sold eight of his highly expensive Perpetuelles and twenty-five other watches of various types. However, by then the Revolution was making Breguet's life in Paris increasingly difficult, and his connections with royalty put him in danger of arrest. In August he managed to obtain a passport, and left for Switzerland with his son and sister-in-law.

Life in Switzerland was by no means easy. Locals were suspicious of refugees, and shortages of watchmaking materials and tools made it difficult for Breguet to continue his business. In Paris, Breguet's workshop in the Quai d'Horloge, which had been managed by his foreman, was confiscated and his property sold. What was worse, he lost not only his house but most of his skilled workmen and equipment. Return to Paris was impossible as his passport had expired, and he was declared a traitor and royalist.

'Secret Signature'

Breguet eventually settled in Neuchâtel and established a workshop there. Later, a second workshop was started in Locle, where he began producing watches for the English and Russian courts. During this time he devised his so-called 'secret signature' to protect himself from forgeries that were beginning to circulate: his friend, Jean-Pierre Droz, made a small pantograph machine that could produce a signature scratched on to the surface of the dial enamel –

Breguet's secret signature.

this was so small that it was almost invisible to the naked eye.

Return to Paris

By 1795 the worst excesses of the 'Terror' were passing, and Breguet could make plans for his return. Tools, particularly files, were in short supply, and he collected all the equipment and materials he could in Switzerland, ready to restart production in Paris. Although Paris was in an economic crisis and food was in short supply, Breguet decided it was safe to return in April. He found trade at a virtual standstill, but as the government needed someone to reorganize the watch and clock industry, in particular to supply the armed forces, he could drive a hard bargain for his services. The government agreed to return his house and works at the Quai d'Horloge, to refit his workshop, and exempt his employees from military service.

Breguet had used his three years in Switzerland to plan all kinds of new mechanisms and projects that he was now able to realize. The years that followed his return to Paris were the most brilliant and productive of his career, cementing his reputation as the leading horologist of his time. He was able to attract the most skilled craftsmen, and the team he assembled was capable of working to the incredibly high standards he insisted on; many of the young men he trained went on to establish some of Europe's leading businesses, including John Roger Arnold. Soon his list of clients included most of Europe's royal families and aristocracy – transcending political constraints, both Napoleon and the Duke of Wellington owned his watches.

The Souscription Watches

Breguet had been criticized for spending too much of his energies pandering to the taste of wealthy clients for ever more ingenious and complicated products; however, one of the schemes he planned in Switzerland for a new, simple but elegant high-grade watch at an affordable price, became one of his most successful ventures.

Breguet's workshop on the Quai d'Horloge.

The Souscription watches could be ordered with a down payment of 25 per cent, and the rest paid off in instalments; around 700 of these watches were sold. The example shown here is a simple single-handed watch with a ruby cylinder escapement, and has Breguet's parachute shock protection (*see* Part I). Another type of watch developed from his time in Switzerland was the 'montre à tact': this model has an external hour hand on the case front, and it was possible to use this to tell the time by feeling its position with regard to touch pieces round the edge of the case. This was a simpler way of telling the time in the dark than with a repeating watch, and it was even possible to use it whilst it was in the wearer's pocket.

Breguet's watches were always characterized by their restrained good taste. The example shown here was sold in 1796 and has several typical features – the silver engine-turned dial

Breguet 'Souscription' watch.

Breguet 'montres à tact'.

Breguet quarter repeating watch, 1796.

showing the age and phases of the moon with a state of wind indicator, and the elegant blued steel hands, which became universally known as 'Breguet hands'.

The Tourbillon

Throughout his career Breguet continued with experiments to improve the timekeeping of his watches. He experimented with several different escapements, including the cylinder, spring detent and lever, as well as developing more than one entirely new design, although none of these was generally adopted by other makers. One of his most notable inventions was the tourbillon, to reduce the effects of positional error (*see* Part 1). He constructed a carriage that contained the balance and escapement; this rotated slowly, generally once per minute, and was intended to average out the different positions of the balance.

The tourbillon is a very difficult thing to construct: it must be of very light construc-

tion to avoid friction on the gearing, yet rigid enough to damp down any vibration. It has been considered the greatest example of the watchmaker's art and is spectacular in operation, yet some wonder whether it has any noticeable effect on the timekeeping of the watch – Baillie comments that 'the time and skill spent on the tourbillon might be better employed in perfecting an ordinary watch'. No doubt it was a good talking point for his clients who were fortunate enough to possess such a marvel of ingenuity!

The Sympathiques

Perhaps the most decadent of all Breguet's productions are the Sympathiques. George Daniels describes them as 'a jewel of misplaced ingenuity in a forest of scientific endeavours'. Only a handful were made, and they were the last word in luxury timepieces. They were a combination of a highly accurate clock and an elegant watch that was housed in a cradle above the clock dial.

Breguet tourbillon watch.

Breguet's 'Duc D'Orléans Sympathique'.

The docking watch for Breguet's Sympathique.

The Marie Antoinette.

When the wearer took off his watch, he (or his manservant) placed the watch in the cradle, whereupon the clock wound the watch and set it to time automatically.

The 'Marie Antoinette'

The most famous of all Breguet's watches is the so-called Marie Antoinette. It is said to have been commissioned by an unknown admirer of the ill-fated queen in 1783, who stipulated that it should contain every known complication, and that wherever possible the parts should be made from gold. It appears to have been an on-going project for Breguet and his staff for over thirty years; Breguet's talented pupil Michel Weber was responsible for most of the work — it is recorded that he was paid 7,250 francs for 725 hours work between 1812 and 1815. By the time it was finished in 1820 it had cost 16,864 francs.

The complications include Perpetuelle winding, equation of time, perpetual calendar, minute repeating, thermometer and state of wind indicator; most of the plates and bridges are made from pink gold, all the friction surfaces are jewelled with sapphire, and the front and back are made from rock crystal to display the working parts. George Daniels writes that 'if ... Breguet intended the watch as a monument to eighteenth-century horology he could not have produced a more fitting tribute.' Breguet died in 1823 at the age of seventy-seven whilst serving as a juror in the Paris Exhibition.

THE DECLINE IN FRENCH WATCHMAKING

Breguet's workshop was the high point of French watchmaking; after his death the firm continued, but increasingly using Swiss movements.

Breguet portrait, 1816.

No French manufacturers followed Japy's pioneering factory watch production of the late eighteenth century. Japy and other manufactures did, however, produce vast quantities of carriage clocks and striking clock movements, which dominated the clock industry in the late nineteenth and early twentieth centuries. English makers were then at the top end of the trade, whilst American and German makers supplied the demand for cheaper, mass-produced clocks. French influence in twentieth-century watchmaking was largely confined to retailing and the fashion industry: the firm of Cartier, and their connection with the Swiss firm of Le Coultre, was a strong influence on watch design throughout the century.

PART III:
THE ENGLISH WATCH INDUSTRY

Tompion watch.

Chapter 11
The Beginnings in England

In the sixteenth century, the main centres of watchmaking were in Germany and France, and little is known of watchmakers working in England at that time. Queen Elizabeth I is recorded to have possessed ten watches and several clocks. Most of those watches were likely to have been French in origin; however, she is known to have had a clockmaker, Bartholomew Newsam, who also made watches. The Metropolitan Museum, New York, has a watch of *c.*1565 that they attribute to Newsam: this is possibly the earliest surviving English watch.

NOTABLE CLOCK- AND WATCHMAKERS

Nicolas Vallin

The first watchmaker in England of whom we have any reliable records is Nicolas Vallin, who emigrated to England around 1590, probably due to religious troubles in the Netherlands. He became the leading clock- and watchmaker in London, and several of his watches have survived. Vallin and his father both died in the London plague epidemic of 1603.

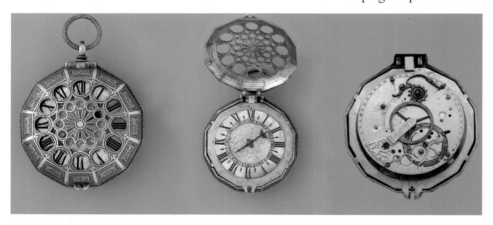

Watch attributed to Bartholomew Newsam, c.1565.

Nicholas Vallin watch c.1600, enamelled with an image of St George; it was probably made for a Knight of the Garter.

Nicolas Vallin gilt brass alarm watch, c.1600.

Michael Nouwen

A Flemish watchmaker, Michael Nouwen, or Nouen, is known to have been working in London around 1600–1610. The clock watch illustrated here is an early type of watch that strikes the hours on a bell attached to the inside of the case.

David Bouguet

David Bouguet was a French Huguenot refugee who settled in London, just outside the control of the City authorities in Blackfriars, an area known as the 'liberties', a place favoured by many Huguenot craftsmen, including engrav-ers and enamellers, where they could trade freely. This competition did not please a group of established London clock- and watchmakers, who objected to their presence in a petition – which included Bouguet's name – to King James I in 1622 to prevent them from trading; the petition failed. Bouguet was one of the founding members of the Worshipful Company of Clock-makers (*see* below), and continued working in London until his death in 1655. The enamelled case of the watch illustrated here, produced in his workshop around 1650, depicts Venus and Adonis.

Clock watch c.1600–1610, by Michael Nouwen, London.

David Bouguet watch, c.1650.

THE WORSHIPFUL COMPANY OF CLOCKMAKERS

English clock- and watchmakers originally belonged to the Worshipful Company of Black-smiths, founded in 1571; like other companies, this one also regulated membership and apprenticeships in the City of London. Many of the growing number of clock- and watchmakers in the early seventeenth century wanted to establish their own company, and despite opposition from the blacksmiths, they succeeded in obtaining a royal charter in 1631 and founded the Worshipful Company of Clockmakers. The charter gave regulatory authority to the clockmakers to control the horological trade in the City of London and for a radius of ten miles around. It incorporated a controlling body that should have had 'continuance for ever under the style and name of The Master, Wardens and Fellowship of the Art and Mystery of Clockmaking'.

However, the clock- and watchmakers of London were not very closely controlled, and it was possible for anyone to set up in business for a small fee. Under these favourable conditions the English trade flourished, and soon the work of London makers rivalled those of France and the low countries, where wars and religious persecution made London a very attractive destination for many talented craftsmen, contributing to the 'golden age' of English horology.

Edward East

One of the founding members of the Clockmakers' Company was Edward East, born in 1602 and baptised at Southill in Bedfordshire. He was apprenticed to Richard Rogers, and was made a freeman of the Goldsmiths' Company in 1627; examples of his early watches confirm that he was a fine craftsman. Despite his young age, he was appointed 'assistant' for life in the new company and became watchmaker to Charles I.

Silver gilt watch c.1640, by Edward East.

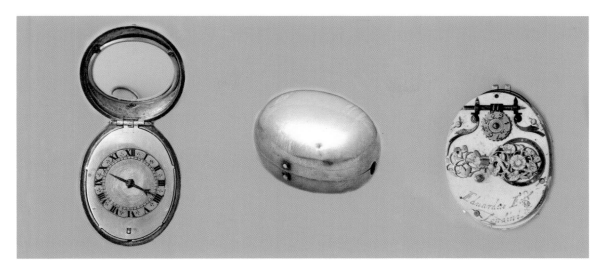

Puritan watch by Edward East, c.1640.

East is first recorded as living in Pall Mall, near the Tennis Court, a convenient place to attend the King, who was said to give one of East's watches as a prize on frequent occasions. He had certainly moved to Fleet Street by 1635 when the King had a gold alarum watch fetched from his premises there. His career was long and successful, and he continued as both clock- and watchmaker until his death at the age of ninety-four in 1696.

During the Commonwealth period, a reaction against earlier extravagant, jewelled pieces gave rise to the 'Puritan watch', a plain, silver-cased timepiece that suited the taste of the times. A good example by East is now in the collection of the Metropolitan Museum of Art in New York.

The portrait by Cornelis Jonson van Cuelen the Younger, a Dutch artist working in England, shows a man in Puritan dress holding such a watch.

Portrait by Cornelis Jonson van Cuelen the Younger, 1657.

Chapter 12
The Golden Age

The restoration of Charles II in 1660 marked a period when England took the lead in scientific advancement; a particular landmark was the foundation of a 'College for the Promoting of Physico-Mathematical Experimental Learning' in November 1660. Two years later the King signed a royal charter, naming it the 'Royal Society of London'. Robert Hooke, who had produced Hooke's Law concerning the properties of the spring in 1660, was appointed Curator of Experiments in 1663.

As discussed in Part I, Hooke and his friend Thomas Tompion were instrumental in one of the most critical developments in watch design:

the application of a spiral spring to the balance wheel.

TOMPION'S BALANCE SPRING WATCHES

The new balance spring watches made at this time rendered all earlier watches obsolete. Now that timekeeping to within a few minutes per day had become possible, a minute hand and even a seconds hand became standard features, making the old single-handed watches appear very crude indeed. Compare the Edward East

THOMAS TOMPION

Thomas Tompion was born to a Quaker family in Northill, Bedfordshire, in 1639. His early life is a mystery, and nothing is known about where he learned his trade; however, we do know that in 1671 he became a Free Brother of the Worshipful Company of Clockmakers with a business in Water Lane off Fleet Street. By then he was already a friend and collaborator of Robert Hooke, and this connection soon led to patronage from the rich and powerful. The quality of his work and attention to detail was legendary, and he inspired a succession of great London makers, including Daniel Quare, George Graham, Daniel Delander and Joseph Windmills. Together they pioneered the use of new, specialized machinery such as wheel- and fusee-cutting machines, producing parts of a precision and beauty of finish unequalled anywhere else.

Thomas Tompion, after the portrait by Sir Godfrey Kneller.

watch on p.99 with the remarkable Tompion watch (below). This is typical of Tompion's work and features the latest improvements, including the balance spring with a regulating device and a stop lever that allows the seconds dial to be used as a timer – surely a very impressive device for a fashionable doctor checking his patient's pulse!

Tompion watch from 1682.

Tompion's fame spread far and wide, to the extent that many forgeries of his watches were soon in circulation, originating mainly in Switzerland. A well-known story circulating at the time tells how a customer brought his watch to the master for repair, whereupon Tompion threw it to the ground and stamped on it, offering the man one of his own: 'Here Sir, this is a real Tompion!' In 1704 he became master of the Clockmakers Company, and in 1708 he went into partnership with his protégé George Graham. It has been estimated that his workshop built around 5,500 watches and 650 clocks.

In 1676 he was commissioned to build two 'great clocks', each with thirteen-foot pendulums beating two seconds, for the new Royal Observatory at Greenwich (replicas can now be seen in the Octagon Room). Such was his fame that on his death in 1713 he was buried in Westminster Abbey; in 1751 his friend and partner George Graham was laid to rest alongside him.

It is frustrating that much more is known about seventeenth-century watchmakers than watchmaking; very few records of working practice or accounts have survived from the period. The workshops of the more successful makers must have been very busy places; in the case of Tompion, the average weekly output from his firm would have been between two and three complete watches, plus one or two clocks per month.

OTHER NOTABLE WATCHMAKERS

Recent research into another successful maker, Charles Gretton (Radage, Meinan & Radage 'Charles Gretton Clock & Watchmaking Through the Golden Age') indicates that his workshop had a similar output in his busiest period. Gretton typically employed five or six apprentices and journeymen, and we can assume that Tompion's workshop was comparable or slightly larger. What is more difficult

Repeating watch by Windmills, London, c.1725 (MMA).

to estimate is the amount of work done outside the main workshop in the form of case making, casting, gilding, engraving and spring making.

We also have evidence of movements and major parts supplied by specialist outworkers such as Benjamin Gray. His daybook records:

> 1707 June 27 Delivered a repeating quarter motion with two springs and a bell to Mr Windmills £11-14-0.

Gray is known to have been a specialist in repeating works, and it was clearly standard practice to send partly made movements to such specialists who fitted certain parts and returned the movements for finishing. We should not think of the makers of the period as working in isolation: London and other centres of watchmaking had an extensive network of highly skilled craftsmen in a multitude of specialisms, and great masters such as Tompion could not have produced the work they did without them.

Chapter 13
The Lancashire Connection and
the Introduction of Machinery

HUGUENOT IMMIGRATION

As a result of sixteenth-century persecution in France, as discussed in Part II, there was a massive migration of French Protestants to England. As a major Protestant nation, England, starting with Queen Elizabeth I in 1562, offered protection to these immigrants, and by 1700 over 40,000 had settled there; French Protestants came to make up some 5 per cent of the population of London.

The Huguenots were talented and industrious, and they brought with them many skills that transformed much of Britain's industry, including silk weaving and glassmaking. It has been estimated that over half of French watchmakers were Huguenots, and many settled in Geneva as well as London; we have seen that some of the earliest watchmakers recorded in the city were part of this dispersion. However, the question is – did some of them settle in South Lancashire?

WATCHMAKING IN LIVERPOOL

There is evidence that watchmaking was established in Liverpool very soon after London. At the same time, Huguenot silk weavers were settling in Norwich, and glassmakers from the Lorraine found Stourbridge a suitable place to set up in business. If Huguenot artisans did move north, might the Liverpool area seem attractive?

Several Lancashire towns close to Liverpool, particularly Prescot, had, since the sixteenth century, been renowned for tool making, in particular for the files that were so important in watchmaking; indeed, the town had a monopoly in England for making high-quality files. Prescot appears to have been sympathetic to immigrants, and their parish records show regular charitable collections for French Protestants during the seventeenth century; a Huguenot named Woolrich is mentioned in the Prescot registers, although there is no evidence to connect him to the watchmaking industry.

Toxteth Park in Liverpool was strongly Puritan, and it is perhaps no coincidence that the first recorded horological artisans in the area lived there, although we have no idea where they learned their trade; we might speculate that Huguenot watchmakers had settled there in the late seventeenth century. Names that we do have were all Puritans; these included a certain Thomas Aspinwall, clearly a man of substance, who died in 1624 and left in his will 'In Work Lofte – Tooles, watch works and watch stuffe', valued at £10; he also left £180, and was owed £165. Aspinwall had an apprentice named James Horrocks, whose son Jeremiah became an eminent astronomer. Despite his early death at just twenty-two, he was the first to predict the transit of Venus in 1639.

Significantly, both the Aspinwall and Horrocks families had the means to send their second sons to the universities of Oxford and Cambridge respectively. Another watchmaker from Toxteth Park, Samuel Midgeley, was given the freedom of the City of Liverpool in 1630. Thus it seems that the watch trade was well established in Liverpool very soon after London, and that Prescot, just ten miles away, with its abundance of skilled labour and an established tool-making industry, would be in a strong position to share in the growing trade.

THE LANCASHIRE-TO-LONDON WATCH TRADE

Prescot was on the route from Liverpool to London, which was well established by the sixteenth century, and much improved by the construction of new turnpikes in the eighteenth century. Good transport would have been essential to trade, and sending small items of high value safely between Lancashire and London was not a problem. Soon Prescot and the surrounding villages maintained an increasing population of horological craftsmen, working from houses with a workshop on the top floor to catch the light, perhaps with an apprentice, producing watch and clock parts or complete movements.

There is increasing evidence that Lancashire watchmakers were selling complete movements to the London trade as early as the turn of the eighteenth century. A recently discovered notebook in the Liverpool archive, containing eighty-four pages of notes and accounts from 1713 to 1756, is a goldmine of information on the local watch trade (*Antiquarian Horology*, December 1985, article by Alan Smith). The book belonged to Richard Wright of Cronton, near Prescot; Wright appears to have been a local landowner who was also engaged in the watch business. He probably employed several artisans and rented a third-floor workshop of a building in the village.

The book details all kinds of work and transactions locally, and it also has references to work done for prominent London makers. Between 1713 and 1715 Wright supplied thirty-one watch movements at an average price of £1 15s 0d to Charles Goode of The Strand, London. Entries for 1721–22 detail work done for Stephen Horseman, who was in partnership with Daniel Quare. Over the period, fourteen watches were sent from London to Wright to be worked on; a typical entry is:

> September ye 19th 1721. Receive'd from Mr Horseman a watch to finish No. 5076. Return'd Oct ye 12.

This is most surprising, as it was assumed that the normal procedure was to supply rough movements to be finished in London; it shows that Quare and Horseman were selling watches

Watchmaker's house in Prescot (nineteenth-century photograph).
ARK, LIVERPOOL ARCHIVES
© KNOWSLEY ARCHIVE SERVICE

with Lancashire-finished movements, perhaps due to pressure of work at busy times. In the eighteenth century the regular coach service from Warrington to London took about eight days, so a turnaround time of a month or so for working on movements was quite possible. Other famous names appearing in the notebook are John Ellicott and Joseph Windmills, two of the most eminent London makers of the early eighteenth century.

If we are to accept that Wright was not unique, it is reasonable to assume that other Lancashire artisans were working for London masters on a regular basis. As wage rates in the north would have been considerably lower than in London, it would be good business sense not only to purchase movements from Lancashire, but to send work north. It is a sad reflection on the times that many of the beautiful watches prominently signed by London makers were largely the work of anonymous Lancashire craftsmen. We can, however, console ourselves with the thought that horological workers were well paid by local standards and were rightly proud of their élite status and fine workmanship.

SPECIALIST HOROLOGICAL PROCESSES

As in any trade, specialists in certain horological processes tended to keep to themselves their methods and the special tools and machinery they had devised. Passing on these 'trade secrets' to their apprentices was part of the deal with parents, who paid well for the training, as this ensured a son's future in a well-paid occupation.

Wheel cutting was one of the most important processes in horological work; from the earliest times, mechanical aids were used to mark out the positions of teeth on a wheel

blank before hand filing. A device called a dividing plate was used: this was a metal disk with a series of holes or indentations for various wheel counts, and it would be linked to the wheel blank for marking out.

It would have been an obvious next step to build a machine incorporating a dividing plate that held a wheel blank, and position it for a rotating cutter to form each tooth. Recent research by Anthony Turner (*Antiquarian Horology*, December 2019, p.514) has uncovered evidence for wheel-cutting machines in the seventeenth century. Letters between Nicholas Toinard and John Locke in 1680 concern the purchase of a wheel-cutting machine; two main types are described both for clocks and watches: the first uses files, and the second uses wheels for cutting – the latter was said to be the more accurate. Tompion is mentioned as having one of his own design, which was a very large machine, fixed in his house and not transportable.

From this it would seem that by the late seventeenth century, wheel-cutting machines using rotary cutters were in regular use. The earliest detailed illustrations of watchmaking machinery come from the *Diderot Encyclopédie* of 1775;

Dividing plate, nineteenth century.

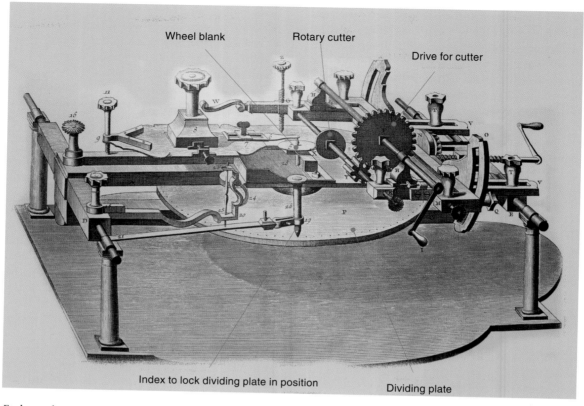

Eighteenth-century wheel-cutting machine.

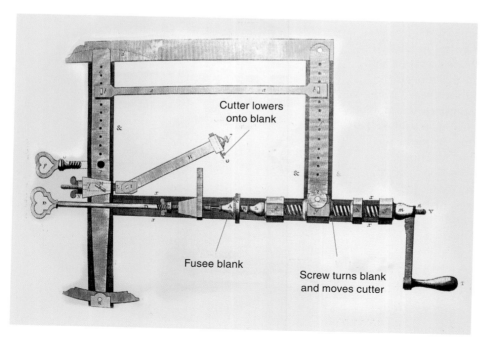

Eighteenth-century fusee-cutting tool.

although somewhat later, these tools would probably have been similar to the wheel-cutting machines Tompion and his contemporaries would have used. Similarly, the fusee-cutting tool illustrated would probably be something like those used in the late seventeenth century.

John Carte, a watchmaker from Coventry, who worked in London from the mid-1690s wrote as follows:

> The English… have invented that Curious Engine for the Cutting the Teeth of a Wheel, whereby that part of the work is done with an exactness which farr exceeds what can be performed by hand: Then there is an engine for equalling the balance wheel: Likewise the Engine for cutting the turns of the fusie: and lastly the instrument for drawing of the steel pinion wier: All which ingenious inventions were first conceived and made at Liverpool in Lancashire in England.
>
> (Manuscript by John Carte – Bodlean Library, Oxford)

Pinion wire.

Pinion wire was made like other forms of wire, by drawing metal rods through a series of hardened steel dies. Special dies were produced with holes in the shape of gear teeth to form lengths of steel pinion of various sizes and teeth numbers; pinion wire could be cut to the lengths required for watch and clock pinions and arbors (*see* Part I). This is further evidence of the vital part played by the Lancashire tool-making industry in the early history of English watchmaking.

Chapter 14
English Pre-Eminence

From the late seventeenth century England was fortunate to have a number of great, inventive clock- and watchmakers, together with scientists and a network of toolmakers; this gave them a decisive advantage over their French rivals.

Daniel Quare, a Quaker, active from 1671, invented the repeating watch, a very useful device at a time when lighting a candle with a tinder box was the only way to tell the time at night. These watches chimed out the time on bells in the back of the case at the depression of the pendant on the top of the watch; usually the hour and quarter, but later to half-quarters

and eventually to the nearest minute. Repeating watches were soon copied by continental rivals, and it is a tribute to Quare's fame that a number of forgeries survive with his name engraved on them.

GEORGE GRAHAM

In the first half of the eighteenth century the outstanding figure in both clock- and watchmaking was George Graham (1673–1751). He came from his native Cumberland to London in 1688 to begin an apprenticeship with Henry

Bell inside case

Hammer

George Graham repeating watch, 1719.

Portrait of George Graham with his 'regulator' clock.

lengthening and shortening of the pendulum rod in changing temperatures; and the development of the recoil-free 'dead-beat' escapement.

His most important contribution to watch technology was the development of the cylinder escapement (*see* Part I) in 1726. It was an improvement on the earlier verge escapement, and probably originated with experiments in Tompion's workshop; he used the escapement in all his later watches, although most makers continued producing verge watches until well into the next century.

The cylinder escapement had the advantage of being much more compact than the verge, later enabling French and Swiss makers to develop their slim, fashionable 'Lepine calibre' watches from the late eighteenth century (*see* Part II). Graham was one of the first watchmakers to use jewelled bearings after Nicholas Facio's patent in 1704 (*see* Part I).

Known at the time as 'honest George', Graham appears to have been a man of great gen-

Aske, and in 1695 went to work with Thomas Tompion, who appears to have treated him like a son. He was clearly a young man of exceptional talent and intelligence, becoming Tompion's partner in 1708 and a leading figure in the Clockmakers' Company.

His interest in astronomy led to his appointment as a Member of the Royal Society in 1721, and he developed a number of instruments for the Greenwich Observatory, the most important being a new, highly accurate type of clock – later known as a 'regulator', capable of keeping time to a few seconds per month. To achieve this, he made two important improvements: a new kind of pendulum using a glass jar containing mercury, which compensated for the

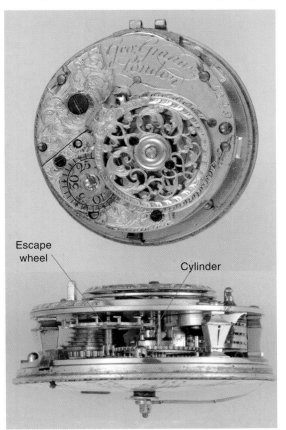

Escape wheel

Cylinder

George Graham watch with cylinder escapement.
PIECES OF TIME

erosity and integrity, willing to share his ideas with other makers who might have been rivals. One morning in 1727 or 1728, he had a visit from a somewhat suspicious Yorkshireman who was in London attempting to get support for his ideas on making a new sea clock. He was John Harrison, who had been sent to Graham by the astronomer Edmund Halley, and he was probably worried that Graham might steal his ideas. Harrison later wrote:

> Graham began, as I thought rather roughly with me... which... occasioned me to become rough too, but however, we got the ice broke... and indeed, he became as at last, vastly surpris'd at the Thoughts or Methods I had taken.

In fact the two men continued their discussion well into the evening, and after giving him dinner, Graham sent Harrison away with an interest-free loan of £200 to return to Yorkshire and begin his work on the great project that consumed him for the next forty years.

THE USE OF JEWELS IN WATCH TECHNOLOGY

As discussed in Part I, the introduction of jewel bearings was a significant step forward in watch technology, and the use of jewels was largely confined to England for most of the eighteenth century. This was not only the result of Facio's patent, but the fact that the source of the raw material — ruby and sapphire from Sri Lanka and Burma — was under the control of the British East India Company. London was the main centre of production for watch jewels well into the nineteenth century, where even American manufacturers such as Waltham were obliged to purchase them.

Chapter 15
Precision Timekeeping

From the late seventeenth century, English watches were renowned for their quality. After the introduction of the balance spring, they had steadily improved in timekeeping, and an error of a few minutes per day was quite satisfactory for most people. However, although clock timekeeping was coming along in leaps and bounds, thanks to the genius of Tompion and Graham, watches lagged well behind.

Hogarth, A Rake's Progress: *Tom Rakewell in the madhouse.*

IMPROVING PORTABLE TIMEPIECES

The main incentive to improving the precision of portable timepieces was quite simply money. As discussed in Part I, there was an urgent need to find a solution to the longitude problem to improve navigation: the offer of payments of up to £20,000 to anyone who could solve the problem seems to have gripped the nation and would have been a regular topic of coffee-house conversation. Such a massive prize attracted not only some of the best minds of the age, but all manner of cranks and chancers with crazy schemes, even a form of insanity: 'longitude lunacy' was a popular subject of satirists. In Hogarth's *A Rake's Progress* the final scene shows Tom Rakewell in the madhouse, surrounded by the unfortunate inmates; these include two 'longitude lunatics', one gazing at the stars through a paper telescope, while the other, in the background, covers the wall with fantastical drawings.

John Harrison and H4

The problem was that no clock existed that could withstand the rigours of sea travel and keep time to within a few seconds per day. Many clockmakers in both England and France took up the challenge, but it was the self-taught Yorkshire clockmaker and carpenter, John Harrison, who, as we have seen, with the encouragement of George Graham and the assistance of some of the best London watchmakers, finally succeeded in producing what was in fact a large watch: his fourth sea clock, known now as H4.

H4 performed brilliantly, keeping time to better than one second per day over a transatlantic voyage; however, it was far too complicated and difficult to make to be produced economically. Nevertheless some of Harrison's developments – illustrated in Part I – and in particular his temperature compensation, transformed the accuracy of future watches. But as we have seen, it was two talented English makers, John Arnold and Thomas Earnshaw working in the 1770s, who improved on Harrison's inventions and began producing not only marine chronometers but wonderful pocket chronometers.

Pocket chronometers were too expensive to capture more than a very limited share of the market, and most people were happy with the traditional verge watches, which continued to be produced in large numbers.

Thomas Mudge and the Lever Escapement

One of the most talented of all English watchmakers was Thomas Mudge (1715–1794). He was apprenticed to George Graham and set up in business at 151 Fleet Street in 1748. He soon became recognized as one of the leading makers of his day, and specialized in watches with advanced complications. Commissions came from royal customers, including Ferdinand VI of Spain for whom he produced at least five watches, one of which was a minute repeater.

During the 1750s Mudge began work on what would be his most lasting legacy, a new detached escapement. All earlier watch escapements interfered with the free swinging of the balance wheel, which limited the accuracy of the watch, but his new lever escapement

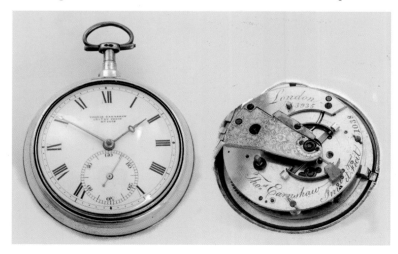

Pocket chronometer: Thomas Earnshaw, c.1790.

Thomas Mudge cylinder watch, 1755.

Thomas Mudge.

(*see* Part I) allowed the balance wheel to rotate almost entirely without interference.

By 1770 he had advanced the design of the escapement to the stage where it could be incorporated into a watch. One such was purchased by King George III and presented to Queen Charlotte, and it is still in the Royal Collection. The lever escapement, with a few minor improvements, eventually became an outstanding success: it was robust, easy to manufacture,

and with the new temperature-compensated balance developed by Arnold and Earnshaw, became the standard for almost all high-grade watches.

The John Arnold Pocket Chronometer

An example of the finest English craftsmanship is the 1781 John Arnold pocket chronometer (which sold for £557,000 in 2016) shown here. It has his 'S'-type temperature-compensated balance with a pivoted detent escapement and helical balance spring. It is interesting to compare it with the Mudge cylinder watch from twenty-five years earlier, and to note that precision now takes precedence over elaborate decoration: these new watches look forward to an age when the best were true scientific instruments.

John Arnold chronometer watch, 1781.

Chapter 16
The Nineteenth Century

THE COVENTRY INDUSTRY

Whilst London makers tended to concentrate on high quality watches for the nobility and the fast-growing merchant class, the focus of larger-scale production of more modestly priced watches moved to Coventry. From the 1770s, what became known as the Coventry or factory apprenticeship system was introduced. In London and Lancashire, the traditional watch finisher's apprenticeship of seven years continued, by which time the apprentice would be considered fully skilled with a good knowledge of the trade and employable as a journeyman, perhaps setting up in business himself if he could raise the capital.

Although some makers, such as Richard Rotherham, produced high quality watches, many Coventry makers simply trained their apprentices in just one of the many aspects of finishing, and continued to employ these men

at apprentice rates, rather than paying journeymen to do the same job. This form of division of labour made it possible to produce basic verge watches at a lower cost than in Lancashire, and some factories had over thirty 'apprentices'. The result was that in the last quarter of the eighteenth century, Coventry-made watches dominated the cheaper end of the market, although these makers rarely signed the movements; most had fictitious names of London or Liverpool makers.

Watchmaking continued to be a major source of employment in Coventry throughout the nineteenth century: the 1851 census records that 776 heads of households were engaged in the watch trade, and the total number of people employed in the trade was over 2,000; it has been estimated that 28 per cent of apprentices were in watchmaking. The most successful Coventry firm was Rotherham & Sons, originally Vale & Co., who leased premises in

Rotherham advertisement, 1885.

the city in 1776, and were trading as Rother-ham & Sons by 1841. The firm took part in the 1851 Great Exhibition, and it was reported that:

> Messrs. Rotherham & Sons, of Coventry, whose establishment was the only one of the kind in England in which machinery impelled by steam power was employed for performing many of the processes in the completion of a watch, exhibited the various parts of a lever watch in the progressive stages of manufacture. All were shown as roughly cast, then as formed into proper shapes, and lastly, as finished. Several movements were also shown, and a beautiful display of 137 watches of all kinds, from the plainest silver watch, to the most elaborately finished and ornamental gold watch.

In 1851 Charles Dickens' magazine *Household Words* printed an article by Harriet Martineau about a visit to Rotherham's factory. From her description it appears that most of the manufacturing of movements was done in the factory, although some 200 outworkers made parts in their homes. Production was about 180 per week, and the price ranged from £3 to £35 for finished watches.

In 1880 the works manager was sent to America to purchase machinery from the American Watch Tool Co., and by 1890 they were making 100 watches per day with 400 to 500 workers, plus about 200 outworkers; this would have made them by far the largest watch manufacturer at that time in Britain. In 1887 G.M. Whipple, superintendent of the Royal Observatory at Kew, wrote of the factory:

> To give you an idea of the extent to which watch production was being pushed in this establishment, and worked by girls and women, I would state that, having adjusted the machinery for the production of one size and class of watch, they were constructing them in batches of 13,000 at a time, and the place was filled with boxes about the size of a tea chest, each full of one single component part of a watch.

Rotherham watch, c.1900.

The Rotherham & Sons factory in 1910.

After 1900 the firm diversified into making bicycle parts and motor accessories; they carried on producing watches during World War I, but by the 1920s were importing Swiss movements. Later they took on the British agency for Buren and Ulysse Nardin.

LANCASHIRE PRODUCTION

The watchmakers and toolmakers of Liverpool and Prescot continued to flourish during the eighteenth century, dominating the English watch industry. The trade depended on Lancashire for the supply of movements and parts for finishing, as well as tools and machinery. Keeping up with the latest developments, they were early users of the new crucible steel invented by the Yorkshire clockmaker Benjamin Huntsman. In the 1740s, Huntsman, a devout Quaker, set up in business near Sheffield smelting iron with coke at very high temperatures in clay pot crucibles. This revolutionary process made steel that was superior to the sheer steel then imported from Germany; however, the Sheffield cutlers were slow to take it up, and it was the Lancashire tradesmen who first learned to forge, harden, temper and polish the new material.

West Lancashire was well placed to be the hub of precision tool making; steel made from iron imported from Sweden was transported across the Pennines to Prescot, and the finished products would then be shipped from Liverpool to America or transported around Britain and Europe. The Sheffield steel makers dominated world production of crucible steel for a remarkably long period, and supplied the Swiss and American manufacturers with steel for most of the nineteenth century. This was made possible by securing the supply of the best iron – an article in *The Rural Cyclopedia* in 1849 explained that:

> Every kind of iron is not suited to the manufacture of steel. English iron does not answer at all. The iron which answers best is made at Danemora, in Sweden, from the magnetic iron ore. The whole of the yearly produce of the Danemora mines, amounting to 8,000 tons, is imported into Britain and converted into steel.

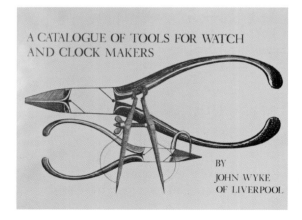

A Prescot watch and tool maker, John Wyke set up business in Liverpool in 1758 and published one of the first mail-order tool catalogues, illustrating the superior quality of Lancashire-made tools and small files that were essential to the watch trade.

Another tool-making firm, Peter Stubbs & Co. of Warrington, became the largest suppliers of tools and dominated the trade though the nineteenth century. With access to the best raw materials, tools and machinery, together with a large, skilled workforce with a long tradition of high-quality work, the artisans of Prescot and its surroundings were in a prime position to produce anything their customers required, from rough movements and parts to fully finished watches and chronometers. In 1795, Dr J. Aitken wrote a description of the country around Manchester; he describes Prescot thus:

> …as the centre of the manufacture of watch tools and movements, of which we shall proceed to give an account. The watch tools here have been excellent beyond the memory of the oldest watchmakers; and the manufacture has been much extended by improvements in making new tools of all sorts, and the invention for first cutting teeth in wheels, and afterwards for finishing them with exactness and expedition. The drawing of pinion wire originated here, which is carried as far as to fifty drawings, and the wire is completely adapted for every size of pinion to drive the wheels of watches, admirable for truth and fitness for the purpose, but left for the workmen to harden… They make here small files, the best in the world, at a superior price, indeed, but well worth the money, from the goodness of the steel and exactness of cutting.

NEW ESCAPEMENTS

Whilst the traditional verge escapement, because of its simplicity and reliability, remained the standard for most watches well into the

John Wyke Liverpool tool catalogue, mid-eighteenth century.

nineteenth century, newer, more sophisticated escapements became available from the mid-eighteenth century for higher-priced pieces. George Graham's cylinder escapements were taken up by both English and French makers later in the century. It was a particularly popular design with the fashion-conscious French as it was very compact and allowed the production of much slimmer watches.

Later in the nineteenth century the Swiss industry produced vast numbers of cheap cylinder watches designed for women, undercutting the English trade and resulting in bitter complaints and accusations of the use of child labour. The duplex escapement (*see* Part I), developed in France by Pierre LeRoy, became popular in high quality watches in the early nineteenth century in its final form, patented in 1782 by Thomas Tryer.

Although it was considered an improvement on the cylinder escapement and it was adopted by some makers in the early nineteenth century, the frictional rest duplex escapement was inherently inferior to the detached lever and chronometer escapements. It was later adopted by the Waterbury Watch Company, USA, in the 1890s for their Waterbury watch, mass produced in their state-of-the-art factory in Waterbury Connecticut, and sold for $2.50.

Another escapement type that achieved some popularity in the early nineteenth century was the rack lever (*see* Part I), developed in France but patented by Peter Litherland, a Liverpool watchmaker, in 1792.

McCabe watch with duplex escapement, 1838. PIECES OF TIME

It was taken up by other Liverpool makers such as Robert Roskell, and was successfully exported to America. The watches were reported to be reliable and gave good service despite being unpopular with the repair trade, as they were tricky to set up; it was soon superseded by the detached lever.

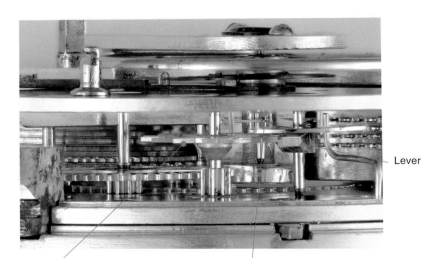

Lever

Rack lever detail. PIECES OF TIME

Escape wheel

Balance pinion

The Dominance of the Detached Lever Escapement

Thomas Mudge, the inventor of the escapement around 1755, seems to have lost interest in it after producing just a handful of pieces, culminating in the Queen Charlotte watch in 1770. He spent his final years concentrating on marine chronometers. Among the English makers who produced early examples of lever watches was Josiah Emery (1725–1794) who made, with the assistance of the escapement maker Richard Pendleton, over thirty, including watches for George III, and one that was presented to Lord Nelson, who was wearing it when he was killed in the Battle of Trafalgar. The British Museum has an example made in 1786 with an Arnold-type 'double S' compensated balance.

One of the improvements that made the lever escapement more reliable was the introduction of 'draw' (*see* Part I) by John Leroux (1744–1817), who became a freeman of Clockmakers Company in 1781. A watch in the Science Muse-

um, London, made by Leroux in 1785 with lever escapement, is the earliest known example that provides draw. Although further refinements were made in Paris by Breguet, the difficulty of making the escapement at first confined production to high-cost precision watches.

However, from the 1830s the movement makers in Lancashire were taking up the challenge and were soon producing watches for the London trade, and the typical Prescot-made 'English lever' watch dominated the trade for the rest of the century.

The original type was the 'full plate' design; later in the century the 'three-quarter plate' type was developed; this was somewhat slimmer and easier to service, although for cheaper watches the full plate type continued to be produced well into the twentieth century.

By the late nineteenth century, the 'going barrel' type of movement that dispensed with the fusee was adopted; also keyless works (*see* Part I) were introduced, enabling slimmer cases and easier winding and hand-setting.

Early English lever by Henry Cole, 1824.

Full plate English lever.

Three-quarter plate English lever.

Late nineteenth-century English 'going barrel' design with keyless work. FELLOWS

For most of the nineteenth century, until American machine-produced watches ruined the trade, the Lancashire makers, particularly those in the Prescot area, prospered as never before. The town was filled with busy workshops covering every aspect of watch and chronometer production, destined for home and export markets. The photograph shows two watchmakers using 'hand throws' or 'turns'; the most important watchmakers' tool used for all kinds of turning and polishing operations.

By later standards, working conditions may seem somewhat primitive, but we must be aware that these were well paid, élite craftsmen capable of producing the finest work to be seen in the elegant London showrooms. Few records of these artisans have come down to us, however we do get an occasional glimpse into their lives. Frank Mercer the chronometer maker, in 1906 wrote the obituary of one of the best known Prescot watchmakers; he recorded that:

> While on a business trip to London, Mr Doke was so disheartened with his poor success that sitting on the church steps in Lombard Street he was compelled to cry; gaining fresh heart, however, he visited Charles Frodsham, who recognising the perfection of his movements, bought his stock and told him to go back and make more. Mr McCabe preferred his movements to all others, and for over 50 years Mr Doke cut practically all the English chronometer wheels.

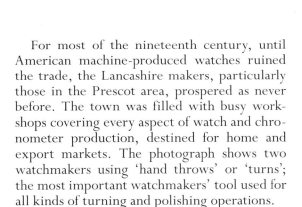

Prescott watchmakers at work. KNOWSLEY ARCHIVE SERVICE

Richard 'Dicky' Doke. © KNOWSLEY ARCHIVE SERVICE

In his book *Watch and Clock Making*, published in 1891, D. Glasgow writes:

> In Mr Wycherley's factory I saw a man making screws in an ordinary hand throw; he turned down the body of the screw, tapped it, rounded the head and cut it off in fifteen seconds… making 1800 screws in a day of ten hours.

COMPETITION FROM AMERICA AND SWITZERLAND

The Great Exhibition of 1851 celebrated the great advances made by British industry, backed by capital generated in a growing empire – including, of course, the profits of plantations employing slave labour. The factory system powered by steam had been developed in Britain, but the highly conservative watchmaking industry resisted mechanization and factory production. Pierre-Frédéric Ingold, a Swiss watchmaker and engineer, had attempted unsuccessfully to set up a factory for the production of watches in Paris, using machines he had been developing for some years.

The enterprise failed after just three years through lack of capital, and Ingold in 1842 moved his machinery to London, where he intended to set up a factory with the support of several noted figures in the trade, including Thomas Earnshaw the younger and John Barwise. However, the 'British Watchmaking Company' never got off the ground in the face of intense opposition from the traditional trade, including a petition to parliament; Ingold was forced into bankruptcy and left the country.

Not all British watchmakers were complacent in the face of growing competition from abroad: Sir John Bennett, a flamboyant character in the City and successful horological retailer, spoke out against the English system and praised the superior education and organization of the Swiss industry, a stance that won him no friends in the trade.

Sir John Bennett – Vanity Fair, *1883.*

He gave many lectures warning of the increasing competition from the Swiss industry, which did not fall entirely on deaf ears: a watch and chronometer maker from Clerkenwell, Edward Daniel Johnson, began lobbying with the purpose of founding a horological institute. His determination paid off, and at a meeting in 1858 at the Belvedere Tavern in Clerkenwell, the British Horological Institute was founded. They stated that:

> The objects for which this Institute is founded are to develop the science of Horology, to foster the arts and various branches of manufacture arising from it, and to stimulate and encourage the production of the best workmanship, by suitable rewards and marks of distinction, and to attain these results by the formation of a library, reading room and a collection of tools, models and machinery, also by the delivery of lectures, and the reading of original papers.

Within a year the institute had moved to permanent premises and had begun publishing the monthly *Horological Journal*, which claims to be the world's oldest monthly technical journal. The BHI has, since then, taken a lead in establishing courses and setting exams and awards in order to further horological training.

During the first half of the nineteenth century America was the biggest export market for English watches, but by the mid-century the Lancashire trade was beginning to suffer from American and Swiss competition, and by the 1880s the trade was in serious decline. An article in the *Prescot Reporter* for September 1885 sums up the situation:

> The watchmakers are finding it dangerous for a town to be dependent on one industry. Until the decline there had been steady prosperity in their trade. Their wages were good and their employment regular. By 1885 the scene had changed, however. Yet such is the condition of the trade in Prescot that during the past ten years nearly half of the watchmakers have been compelled to face the alternative of semi-starvation in their own trade, or find a means of living by adopting the profession of

British Horological Institute arms.

> a soldier or, when it is to be had, a labourer in the coal pits, and many of those who remain only manage to keep the wolf from the door by the exertions of their wives, who go out charring or working in the fields.

During the next year the *Prescot Reporter* printed many letters concerning the depression of the industry, and several meetings were held to attempt to find a solution to the problem. Sir John Bennett weighed in with a speech to the BHI in 1886, pointing out that one million pounds was sent to Switzerland every year for watches that ought to be produced in England.

THE LANCASHIRE WATCH COMPANY

We have seen how in Coventry, Rotherham & Sons had begun machine production in the first modern English watch factory, importing American machinery and developing production lines with women working alongside men, although production was small compared to the huge Waltham and Elgin factories across the Atlantic. In an attempt to remedy the situation in Prescot, the Lancashire Watch Company was formed in Prescot in 1888 – this was the brainchild of T. P. Hewitt, the owner of a small watch factory. A group of local worthies, and also the Earl of Derby, raised start-up capital of £50,000 and sent Hewitt to America to study their methods of machine production.

Part of the capital of the new firm was to be used to purchase the businesses of local movement manufacturers and associated trades, together with their tools and equipment; their workers would then be employed in the new factory. Inevitably this plan met considerable

Lancashire Watch Co. factory. © KNOWSLEY ARCHIVE SERVICE

resistance from many of the older tradesmen, who were opposed to the prospect of retraining and saw the new system as cheapening their high standards of work. However, the dire condition of the trade made it clear that change was inevitable, and many businesses sold out to the company. Altogether over £20,000 was paid out, mostly in shares, to purchase small businesses.

The foundation stone was laid in 1889, and the new factory, which was steam heated and lit by gas, was opened in 1890. An 84-horsepower engine named the 'Horologer' was installed to power the machinery, and by 1893 the workforce numbered around 1,000, both men and women – although the women were expected to leave when they got married.

The Factory Design and Layout

The design and layout of the factory was based on the Elgin Factory in Illinois, which Hewitt had probably visited. Whilst most of the specialized machinery was imported from American firms, many items, such as lathes and slotting machines, came from British manufacturers; in addition, the factory toolroom soon began to adapt and produce special tooling for the factory, often improving on the original American machines. The escape-wheel cutting machine is an example of the new precision tooling: each tooth of the wheel has seven cuts given in turn by the fly cutters, four of steel and three of sapphire for polishing; several steel wheel blanks would be mounted together on the spindle attached to the dividing plate.

LWC finishing shop, c.1900.
© KNOWSLEY ARCHIVE SERVICE

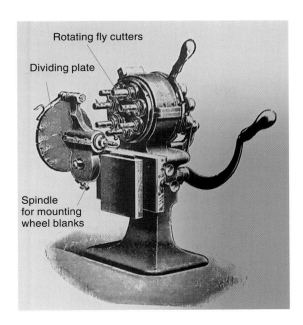

Escape-wheel cutting machine.

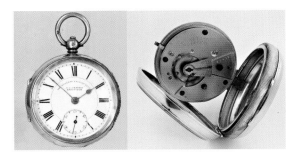

*Lancashire Watch Co. 'The Express English Lever',
1902.*

*Russell keyless watch with LWC three-quarter plate
seventeen-jewel movement, c.1890.*

Factory Production

In the early years the company appears to have
continued producing older style Lancashire
movements, gradually introducing new designs
and improvements, including keyless watches
and three-quarter plate movements, and aban-
doning the older ratchet-toothed escapement
in favour of the American/Swiss-style club-
toothed design with steel escape wheels. A large
range of qualities was available, as described in
an early catalogue:

> We make a full series, from 0 to 18 size of
> stem set watches, in all grades from 7 jewel
> Gilt or Nickel Movements to 23 Jewelled and
> Adjusted Movements of the highest grade.

All movement parts were made in the factory
apart from the mainsprings and balance springs,
which were purchased from Switzerland. Cases
were mostly supplied by outside manufacturers
in Coventry and Birmingham, although from
1895 silver cases were made in the Prescot factory. During the 1890s it is estimated that the
factory was producing around 50,000 watches
per year, compared to Waltham's 500,000 to

1,000,000 and Elgin's around 500,000. Most
of the output went to large retailers, including H. Samuel of Birmingham and Russell of
Liverpool, either in the form of completed
watches or movements; most had no indication
that they were made by the company, and were
either signed by the retailer or sold under various names such as 'The Express English Lever'
or 'Acme Lever'.

Decline and Fall

By the turn of the century sales were flagging,
partly as a result of cheap American watches
flooding the market. In a desperate attempt to
compete, the 'John Bull' model was introduced.
It was advertised as 'The cheapest ENGLISH
WATCH produced' and sold for 5s, about the
same price as the American Westbury 'Dollar
Watch'. The trade price was 3s 9d, or £2 3s 9d
per dozen. The only way to have made this pay
would have been to sell them by the hundred

LWC 'John Bull' model, 1910.

thousand, as were the Westbury watches. In the event the watch was an abject failure, selling only about 5,000 from 1909 to 1911.

The firm was forced to diversify in an attempt to survive, and a range of wall clocks was introduced, the typical English dial clock familiar in offices and schools up and down the country. They were made in five different grades, priced from 23s 9d to 8 guineas for the best quality fusee models. All kinds of engineering products were advertised, including cycle gears, time registers, dies, lathes and various kinds of small mechanisms. The end finally came in 1911 with an auction that included 2,361 lots of tools and machinery; the factory buildings were taken over by the army as barracks during World War I.

LUXURY WATCH PRODUCTION

Whilst some English makers established factories attempting to compete with the Swiss and American watches, others went up-market, producing some of the most complex watches ever made. These masterpieces of the watchmaker's art were made for some of the wealthiest men of the age, including the banker J. Pier-

pont Morgan and the automobile tycoon James Ward Packer; they became a spectacular swansong for English watchmaking.

The firm of Nicole Neilsen was renowned for high-quality watches produced in their works in Soho Square, London. They supplied various complex watches to retailers such as Charles Frodsham, E. J. Dent and Smith & Sons, including chronographs, minute repeaters and tourbillon models. The firm originated in Geneva, where the parent company Nicole & Capt. was founded in 1837 – they opened their London branch in 1843; in 1876, the Danish-born watchmaker Emil Neilsen became a partner. Although some specialized parts came from Switzerland, it seems that most of the work was done in the Soho Square factory.

From 1904 the firm began to diversify, producing instruments and accessories for the new motor industry from their factory in Watford; the watch factory in Soho Square went into liquidation in 1934.

Split-second chronograph by Nicole Neilsen. PIECES OF TIME

Detail of the Nicole Neilsen tourbillon carriage.

Chapter 17
Twentieth-Century Mass Production

SMITHS INDUSTRIES

The firm that dominated the last period of watch manufacture in Britain was S. Smith & Son (later 'Sons'). Samuel Smith opened his first shop in 1851 in Newington Causeway, London, near the Elephant & Castle inn; his son, Samuel Smith Jnr (1850–1932), opened a new shop in 1871 at 85 The Strand, trading as S. Smith & Son. In 1882 a second shop was opened at 9 The Strand, and by the end of the century the firm had become London's leading clock, watch and jewellery retailers. In common with other London retailers, their watches were mostly made in Lancashire and Coventry, although increas-ingly Swiss watches were sold under the Smiths name. A huge range was retailed, from the basic English lever 'Strand' model, retailing at £1 10s 0d, to watches of the highest quality supplied by Nicole Nielsen.

In 1884 a watch was submitted to the new Kew Observatory and received a Class A Cer-tificate – and over the next twenty years Smiths held the accolade of 'best watch of the year' (fitted with Nicole Neilsen movements) no fewer than seven times. The firm was a regu-lar supplier of watches and chronometers to the Admiralty, and watches were provided for both of Captain Scott's Antarctic expeditions. The plain gunmetal-cased pocket watch that was recovered from Scott's body can now be seen at the BHI museum in Upton Hall, Newark, UK.

By the early 1900s Smiths were providing clocks for the new motor-car industry, and in 1904 were granted a joint patent with Robert

S. Smith & Son model 82, 1899.

Watch recovered from Captain Scott's body (in the BHI museum Upton Hall, Newark).

Early Smiths speedometer.

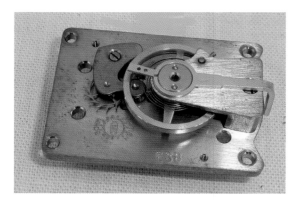

ABEC clock escapement.

North of Nicole Neilsen for Britain's first car 'speed indicator'. These were manufactured in Watford by Nicole Neilsen, who soon expanded into various motor accessories including dynamos and electric motors, as well as the speedometers that were marketed by Smiths.

Smiths opened a new motor accessory works at Great Portland Street, and the watch and jewellery business separated from Smiths (Motor Accessories). With the coming of war, it was clear that demand for all kinds of military equipment would be huge, and Smiths built a new factory at Cricklewood Broadway, London, for their expanding Motor Accessories division: this took on orders for military timepieces and instruments for the new aircraft, including engine speed indicators and eight-day dashboard-mounted clocks using Swiss movements.

The inter-war years were lean times for the watch and jewellery business, and on the death of Samuel Smith in 1932, S. Smith & Sons went into liquidation and was sold to Bravingtons. This left the Motor Accessories division to develop its aircraft and motor-car instrument business. In 1924 Smiths secured an agreement with the French firm of Edmond Jaeger to market their chronometric speedometers, and

eventually gained a controlling share in what became British Jaeger Instruments Ltd. In association with Jaeger, Smiths produced their first complete British-made clocks, mostly for motor vehicles.

The most difficult component to manufacture was the lever platform escapement, and a separate company – ABEC (All British Escapement Company) – was founded to produce them. A new factory, the 'Chronos' works, was completed in 1932 with the installation of Swiss machine tools supplied by LeCoultre, producing car clocks and speedometers; by 1933 some 95 per cent of British cars were fitted with Smiths speedometers and clocks. ABEC escapements were sold to many clock manufacturers, including Mercers for their bulkhead clocks, and production continued until the early 1960s.

WARTIME PRODUCTION

From 1936 the British government began to set up 'shadow' factories to protect vital production in the event of war. These facilities, intended to be secret, included plants for the production of aircraft instruments; the Smiths factory at Cricklewood recruited many Swiss production engineers along with specialized machinery from Switzerland and Germany. A desperate push began to get machinery to Britain before the outbreak of hostilities began. Some German machine tools that had amazingly reached

Dieppe in spring 1940, had to be rescued with the help of the Royal Navy in the teeth of the advancing German forces. It is said that a group of Smiths engineers, at great risk, were dropped by parachute into the Jura region of Switzerland to collect a supply of hair-springs and diamond wire drawing dies from LeCoultre, to be transported home by light aircraft.

In 1939 it was considered necessary to remove production out of range of enemy bombing, and land near Bishop's Cleave, Cheltenham, was purchased and S. Smith & Sons (Cheltenham) Ltd was formed. The first factory, CH.1, was completed by May 1940 for the production of all kinds of vital aircraft instruments; given the lack of high precision machinery, part of CH.1 was involved in the design and manufacture of these tools and a new generation of precision engineers was trained.

A second factory, CH.2, was opened in late 1940 for the production of smaller, more delicate items such as aircraft clocks. CH.2 later became known as the 'watch laboratory' and went on to develop a new range of Smiths watches. By the end of the war the Cheltenham factory had expanded to include a spring-making factory, drawing offices and a training school, in addition to production facilities for all kinds of aircraft instruments.

It is not clear how many military watches Smiths supplied during the war; a number of pocket and wrist watches, including chronographs were provided. Using their connection with Jaeger LeCoultre, movements were imported from Switzerland and cased in England. The export of chronographs was prohibited under the German-Swiss War Trade Agreement of 1941, and it appears that many of these were smuggled into Spain through Vichy France. These watches were generally marked 'S.S.&S'.

POST-WAR PRODUCTION

The Smiths Cheltenham factory had been working on the development of a new wrist watch movement during the latter years of the war. At their AGM in February 1947 it was announced that the manufacture of a new high-grade jew-

elled-lever watch had begun at the Cheltenham factory, and that a new factory was under construction in South Wales for the production of a 'popular watch' – that is, a pin-lever pocket watch. Dennison of Birmingham were contracted in 1946 to produce cases for the new civilian watches. Early 1947 advertisements show three Cheltenham-made models ranging in price from £11 11s 0d to £25 for a 9ct gold-cased model.

In 1945 the Smiths Group joined with Ingersoll to set up a new firm, the Anglo Celtic Watch Company, with a factory in the Welsh village of Ystradgynlais, where both Ingersoll and Smiths Empire pin-lever watches were produced. The Ingersoll watch was developed from the American Waterbury watch, the 'Dollar Watch', assembled in England from imported parts under the 'Ingersoll' brand from the early 1920s. Smiths took over the movement design for their budget-priced pocket-watch range with a starting price of £1 3s 9d; the Empire wrist-watch range retailed from £2 2s 6d.

Smiths watch production was divided

Smiths advertisement from the early 1950s.

between Ystradgynlais where the cheaper pin-lever watches were mass produced, and the high-grade jewelled lever movements that were made in part of the Cheltenham complex alongside the facilities producing aircraft instruments, which were becoming an increasingly important part of the Smiths industrial empire. Smiths clocks were manufactured at their north London Chronos Works.

Advertisement celebrating the ascent of Everest, 1953.

The Smiths fifteen-jewel movement.

The fifteen-jewel movement was used in various forms until the 1970s; the earlier models had plain balance bearings, while this had Kif shock protection, introduced in the early 1950s. The photograph shows the seven-jewel pin-lever movement used in the 'Empire' models, made in the Ystradgynlais factory.

Seven-jewel Smiths Empire movement.

Smiths De Luxe, c.1955.

The Everest expedition in 1953 was issued with thirteen specially prepared Smiths de Luxe watches, and the successful ascent was an opportunity to promote an advertising campaign, although Rolex watches were also issued and Sherpa Tenzing Norgay was probably wearing an Oyster Perpetual. Hillary presented his watch to the Clockmakers Company and it is now to be seen in London's Science Museum.

The advertising of the budget-priced Empire watches featured sporting heroes such as the footballer Stanley Matthews, and pocket watches with character dials such as the cowboy 'Ranger' model were produced in large numbers.

Smiths WWW military model.

Smiths Empire 'Ranger' model.

MILITARY WATCHES

Various plans were made to supply the RAF with watches towards the end of World War II, and there are reports that 2,000–3,000 were made 'under great difficulty'; only a few of these have survived. From 1948 the main standard for military watches was the GS (General Service) model WWW ('Watch Wristlet Waterproof'). Many Swiss makers supplied watches to this specification, and Smiths began developing a British model. The first batch was issued in 1953, based on their civilian De Luxe model, while further contracts were issued in 1954, 1956 and 1960.

AUTOMATIC WATCHES

In 1961 Smiths introduced the Imperial Automatic model based on their nineteen-jewel top-of-range manual movement, with an automatic work that was very similar to the successful IWC design. The stainless-steel model sold for £25, and the 9ct gold model for £50; sales were suspended around 1965, perhaps under threat from litigation by IWC, although this has never been confirmed.

The heyday of British watch production was the mid-1950s; in 1956 2,350,600 were sold, and in 1957 2,596,100 – most of these would be pin levers. The higher-grade watches from the Cheltenham factory had never been profitable and had to be subsidized to compete with Swiss products. The company had a small research facility developing electronic watches, and from 1970 a few quartz watches were produced under the 'Quasar' name; the project was abandoned in 1974.

By the 1960s, watches and clocks had become a small part of the vast range of Smiths Industries' products and services, and in 1970 the loss-making Cheltenham watchmaking facilities were closed down and around 400 remaining workers were made redundant. The Ystradgynlais works briefly took up production of jewelled lever watches, but the quality was inferior to the Cheltenham-made movements, and in 1972 this factory was also closed down, ending British quantity watch production.

Smiths Imperial Automatic model 1962.

PART IV:
THE SWISS WATCH INDUSTRY

Painting 'The Cabinotiers' by Franz von Ziegler, 1879.

Chapter 18
The Beginnings in Geneva

Geneva, the original centre of the watch industry in Switzerland, became a republic in the fifteenth century. As the home of John Calvin, it had become an important centre of the Protestant revolution in the mid-sixteenth century. Like London, Geneva benefited from the influx of Protestant refugees escaping from persecution in the neighbouring Catholic countries, including many skilled watchmakers from France.

Geneva had once had a flourishing jewellery trade, which went into decline under the puritanical regime of Calvin; however, although the vanity of wearing jewellery was condemned, watches were the exception, and the French Huguenot craftsmen took the lead in establishing watch manufacturing in the city. They were keen businessmen and founded a strong export trade, including crucifix watches, prohibited in Geneva, to the Catholic clergy abroad, and astronomical watches for the flourishing Turkish market.

By the early seventeenth century there were enough watchmakers in Geneva to form a guild to regulate the trade, limiting a master as to the number of journeymen he could employ and apprentices he could train. Later in the century there were many complaints that foreign merchants and craftsmen were settling in Geneva and undermining local artisans, engaging in unscrupulous and aggressive trading practices.

Despite a good deal of pressure, the Geneva authorities decided not to expel the immigrants, preferring to ensure that they paid their share of taxes and duties: after all, they were bringing in new techniques to the trade and generat-

Mid-seventeenth-century crucifix watch by Jaques Joly of Geneva.

Geneva watch made for the Turkish market by Stadler c.1630.

A seventeenth-century print of a watchmaker's shop.

ing new business. This enlightened policy was a great success, and by the end of the century Geneva was transformed from a country town with mostly wooden structures to a city of fine stone buildings in the latest fashion.

The district of Saint-Gervais became the centre of watchmaking, and from the early eighteenth century the old wood-framed merchant houses were replaced with tall buildings of five or six storeys; the workshops were located in the upper floors, or *cabinets*, with large windows, and it was here that the craftsmen, known as *cabinotiers*, worked.

ÉTABLISSAGE : A NEW SYSTEM

The process of watchmaking was also being transformed, from the traditional workshop

Watchmaker's bench, nineteenth century.

where a master, who employed journeymen and apprentices, supervised the entire production process, to a new system, known as *établissage*. The *établisseur* – a master watchmaker – gave out raw materials and advanced money to subcontractors who made the various components; he then supervised the assembly and finishing of the watches, selling them either direct to local clients or to merchants for sale abroad.

This form of division of labour created two distinct classes of worker. At the top of the pecking order were the highly skilled artisans, usually citizens and burghers, who did the finishing, assembly and adjustment. Lower down were those engaged in roughing out the plates, pillars and wheels of the watch and the various other components such as dials, chains and springs.

This new class of ancillary workers were often immigrants, and increasingly, peasant farmers looking for work to occupy idle hands in the long winter months. These were mostly dairy-farming people from the mountain regions, not the horny-handed agricultural workers from the arable lowlands, where the rough labour of tilling the soil rendered them unfit for fine work. These dairy-farming families were involved in raising livestock, and many had nimble fingers ideally suited to delicate work. Many farmers were happy to provide pay and board to entice journeymen to come from the city and train their wives and children in the new skills. Although this was strictly against the guild rules, the Geneva masters came to rely on a steady supply of cheap components from the surrounding countryside, and the hill farmers benefited from the extra income.

GENEVA PROSPERS

During the eighteenth century Geneva continued to prosper, and her watchmakers and even journeymen became men of substance, earning more than workers in other trades and enjoying a high standard of living. Fees for apprenticeships were higher in the watch trade: for instance, it cost a father twice as much to have his son trained as a watchmaker than as a goldsmith. This success did not go unchallenged – the French in particular were keen to establish a centre of production in Besançon on the other side of the border, offering Geneva-based craftsmen various inducements including loans, accommodation and exemption from military service to settle there. However, the local Catholic population did not take kindly to the Protestant immigrants, and the new centre was not a success.

Lake Geneva by artist Hubert Sattler.

Chapter 19
Watchmaking in the Jura

By the end of the eighteenth century the Swiss watch industry began to evolve further and had spread to the Jura mountains along the French border, where farming families took to the new work with great energy. Neuchâtel soon began to rival Geneva as a centre of production. The nature of the trade also began to change, with increasing reliance on merchants who would travel abroad to sell the watches. The merchants dictated the terms of trade to the master watch-makers, sometimes making advance payments against sales, or more often paying the makers only when the watches had been sold. Most of the business was done at the great European fairs such as those at Leipzig and Beaucaire, where Swiss-made watches sold at prices that undercut the London and Paris dealers.

INCREASING EXPORT TRADE

Unscrupulous merchants were not above order-ing watches to be made in Switzerland with signatures of well-known London makers. A Geneva merchant, George Achard, purchased a George Prior watch made for the Turkish mar-ket and had 600 copies made for sale in Smyrna at knock-down prices. The development of mer-chant banking enabled the Genevan merchants to finance an expensive selection of watches to take to a major trade fair or for sale to the lucrative markets of the Orient. The high prices paid for watches in countries such as China jus-tified the risks involved in reaching such distant shores.

The Travelling Merchant

However, life for the travelling merchant was not easy, and profits were won at great risk to personal safely. Italy, a hotbed of banditry, was particularly dangerous. J.B. Vacheron, at the end of a particularly hazardous trip in 1818, wrote home to his partner:

> We have encountered from time to time arms and legs nailed to posts, as a sign to travellers that brigands had been executed there because they had committed murder. I confess that this disgusting spectacle would have decided me to turn back if I had been alone; but being with Degrange [a fellow Genevan merchant], and both of us very well armed and resolved to defend ourselves to the death rather than give up our assortments, we did not hesitate to go on ahead... How much do all these reflections and these repeated chances make me want to go home, to lead a peaceful life free of all these tribulations!
>
> To this end, I beg of you, dear friend, not to order any more watches. Be content to fin-ish what is already in the works, and send it to me quickly so that I can, if that's possible, busy myself with placing it. I shudder to think again the sad thoughts that have afflicted me on this latest perilous journey! If I had been stopped and killed – the same thing – on this road, what would my family have become, and my old father who has no one left but me? This thought alone is more than enough to make me swear off travel completely, and I assure you that that is my intention, even if I have to take up the file again.

As good as his word, soon after his return home, François Constantin, an excellent businessman and talented salesman, was taken into the firm and took over the journeys to Italy, relieving Vacheron of the perils of travelling. The part-nership blossomed, and the firm of Vacheron & Constantin celebrated its 250th anniversary in 2005.

A Sea Fight with Barbary Corsairs (Laureys a Castro).

Having run the gauntlet of highwaymen and various banditti, the intrepid merchant who travelled by sea was no safer: he faced the threat of the notorious Barbary pirates en route to the eastern Mediterranean, who, rather than killing their captives, held them for ransom. Swiss watchmakers sent by their employers to work in such places as Constantinople often required their masters to guarantee to pay the going rate for their ransom if captured.

BOOM AND BUST

In the boom years from 1750 to 1785, when the watchmakers of Geneva could sell all they could make, it has been estimated that production exceeded 80,000 pieces per year. How-

ever, the French Revolution and the wars that followed were bad for the trade, and by the turn of the century, the value of the output from Geneva probably halved, and artisans were forced to seek work elsewhere.

The industry in the Jura region, to the north of Geneva, fared no better, and despite attempts by the Republic to prop up the trade, market forces prevailed and production went into a similar decline. The wage levels of the Jura were always lower than in Geneva, and the watches they produced were generally cheaper; despite this, sales languished, and wage levels were reduced further in an effort to undercut the competition. The result was an inevitable sacrifice of quality, and the reputation of Neuchâtel watches suffered badly, leaving Geneva to take the lead in producing more expensive, high fashion pieces.

Efforts to restrict the imports of Swiss watches into France and England encouraged smuggling: watches were easily concealed, and their high value made considerable profits for the contrebandiers of Geneva and Neuchâtel where the state authorities turned a blind eye to the trade – after all, these tiny states had to export most of their production in order to survive.

In 1787 the London Clockmakers Company successfully petitioned the government to impose a heavy import tax on foreign watches and clocks. Members complained that the quality of English work would be debased if they had to try to compete with goods produced with cheap foreign labour, such as the women and children in the Swiss gilding trade. In times of war and revolution trade became increasingly risky; a rare surviving letter from Jonas

Contrebandiers Aragonais — Alfred Dartiguenave.

Berthoud in Paris to his father and brother in Fleurier in 1789 points out the pitfalls of attempting to trade in London:

> …the English place too many obstacles in the way of foreign trade… They have recently ruined several houses by confiscations… You have to keep the goods at friends' houses; you don't dare to carry them about town or show them to people you are not sure of.

THE NEW LEPINE CALIBRE WATCH

From the late eighteenth century, many Swiss makers began to specialize in a new and distinctive style of watch, influenced by developments in France. During the eighteenth century watches were generally worn in a waistcoat or trouser pocket, rather than hung round the neck or on a belt, as in earlier times. Traditional verge watches, favoured by English makers,

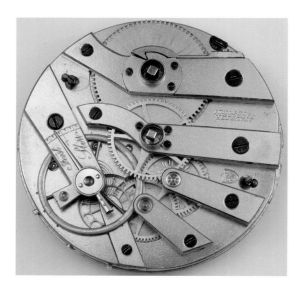

Typical Swiss 'Lepine calibre' movement.

were relatively thick and heavy, not well suited to the modern fashion. In France in particular there was a strong demand from the fashionable set for slimmer watches that would not cause unsightly bulges, and which would slip in and out of the pocket easily. The new Lepine calibre fitted the bill admirably.

The Paris watchmaker Jean-Antoine Lepine (1729–1814) developed the new movement design that made much slimmer watches possible (*see* Part II); this type of movement was taken up with great success by Swiss makers in the early nineteenth century.

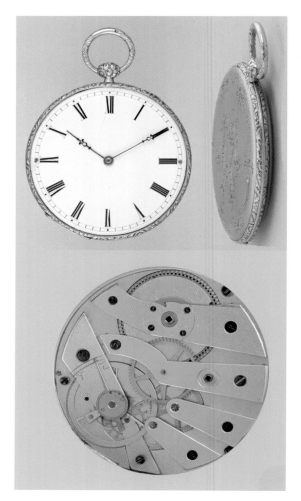

Lepine calibre watch c.1830, signed Mermod Frères Genève.

Chapter 20
Mass Production

FRÉDÉRIC JAPY AND THE JURA INDUSTRY

A native of Beaucourt, then an enclave of the Duchy of Württemberg on the French side of the Jura, Japy (1749–1813) set up in business as a watchmaker in 1771. He earned his living making the rough movements – ébauches – for watchmakers in Neuchâtel. He did well and took on several apprentices, and by 1776 was in a position to expand his business, not in the usual way, but with a single step moving watch production into the factory age. He raised the great sum of 600 Louis d'or and contracted the firm of Jenneret-Gris of Le Locle to build a number of machines to his own design for the manufacture of the standard verge ébauche then in use by the watchmakers in the region.

By the 1780s, Japy's new power-driven factory was turning out over one hundred verge movements per day at two and a half francs each – the equivalent of a day's labour for a working man, and less than a tenth of the value of a finished watch. Within ten years the total annual production was over 100,000, most of which went to the finishing trade in the Jura.

This reliance on movements from across the border was seen as a cause for concern, and in 1793 a factory on the same lines was set up in Fontainemelon by the Benguerel and Humbert families. By 1797 the company employed 120 workers, and in 1841 it was reported that the factory – Fabrique d'Horlogerie de Fontainemelon (FHF) – was supplying most of the movements used by the watchmakers in the cantons of Neuchâtel and Berne.

The ready supply of cheap and uniform movements gave the Jura watch industry a great advantage over its competitors, as the anonymous author of a prize-winning essay for the Genevan authorities on the Neuchâtel industry in 1818 explained:

> …They use the rough movements of Japy for just about every sort of watch. The pieces are all perfectly alike, the parts always matched. As a result, supplies are easily assembled at the lowest possible price, because every part is suited in advance to its purpose and is always made in the same way. As a result it costs less

Statue of Japy in Beaucourt.

Japy movement c.1800.

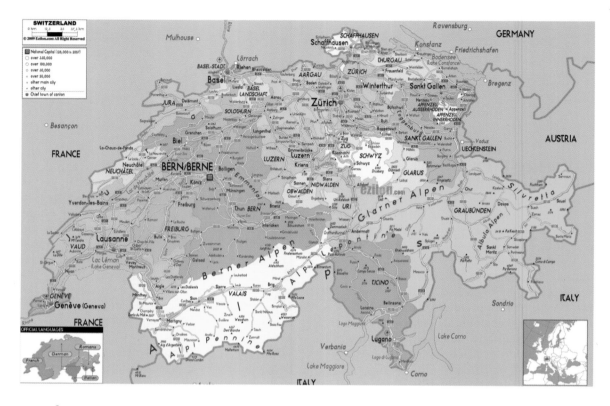

Map of Switzerland.

than ours, which always vary… the worker who works up the rough movement loses no time in examining and contriving… they deliver better watches for less money.

The Swiss industry by the early nineteenth century was now firmly divided into two parts: the Geneva makers concentrated on the higher-priced pieces, leaving the cheaper end of the market to the Jura industry. In spite of having to import the raw materials, including British steel, they could easily undercut and outsell English products, and Swiss wages for skilled workers soon matched those in the English industry.

Novelty Watches

Apart from price, the Swiss industry had the advantage of diversity that enabled them to cater for all markets and to experiment with novelties that pandered to all tastes. Whatever the cus-

tomer required, he could find a local *fabrique* to fulfil his order, however small or large. Certain areas came to specialize in certain types

Watch by Bovet, Fleurier, c.1850, made for the Chinese market.

Repeating watch with concealed erotic painting by Bovet c.1810.

Quarter-repeating automaton watch by Robert & Courvoisier, La Chaux-de-Fonds, c.1810.

of movement: the Vallée de Joux specialized in complicated pieces, Le Locle in chronometers, Fleurier made watches specifically for the Chinese trade, and if you wanted the finest specialist tools, you would go to the Val de Travers. The Chinese market was particularly lucrative around the mid-nineteenth century – these watches often feature centre jump seconds hands and intricate flower enamelled cases.

The makers of Geneva produced a vast range of watches, particularly pieces intended for ornament rather than utility, lavishly set with jewels or with exquisite enamel paintings to suit all tastes. Some of the most expensive were watches that had concealed erotic paintings.

Another lucrative branch of the Geneva trade featured automaton and musical watches. A vast range was produced, showing, amongst other novelties, small moving figures striking bells or tightrope walking, or even a dog barking at a cat, complete with simulated barking noises instead of chimes.

From around 1850, the Swiss were quick to exploit the new demand for small, decorative watches worn attached to a brooch or on a chain around the neck. The simple Swiss 'going barrel' movement with cylinder escapement was easily miniaturized for use in these smaller watches. Fitted in silver, gold or enamel cases, they were instant best-sellers, undercutting the better quality but dull English pieces – fashion triumphing over performance.

Automaton watch with barking dog, Piguet & Meylan, Geneva, c.1810.

Swiss late-nineteenth-century silver fob watch.

RISE AND DECLINE IN SWISS PRODUCTION

Around the mid-nineteenth century, Swiss production was rising rapidly, particularly at the cheaper end of the market. Neuchâtel, for instance, in 1844 produced around 280,000 watches, increasing to 800,000 by 1855, and by 1870 they accounted for about one-third of the entire Swiss output. Mechanized production was increasing, with more water- and steam-powered factories challenging the traditional *fabriques*.

However, despite claims from makers such as Vacheron and LeCoultre that they were able to produce interchangeable parts, the light-weight machinery available at the time was not capable of the leap in precision production required. Equipment needed constant adjust-ment by skilled operatives, and parts required a good deal of hand finishing and fitting to pass muster. This was not a problem in a country with a ready supply of skilled artisans, unlike in America where the absence of such a pool of labour was forcing advances in mechaniza-tion. Swiss exports to the USA reached a peak value of 18.3 million francs in 1872, but by 1876 it had fallen to a mere 4.8 million: clearly, the Swiss had a problem.

AMERICAN SUPERIORITY

The Philadelphia Centennial Exhibition was in 1876, and the Swiss sent Edouard Favre-Perret to investigate the competition that was promi-nently on show. On his return, his report to his compatriots in La Chaux-de-Fonds caused considerable consternation throughout the industry. He not only criticized the Swiss for taking the American market for granted, sup-plying sub-standard products that harmed the reputation of Swiss watchmaking, but also for ignoring the advances in machine production that had been pioneered in the USA. He report-ed that not only was their productivity higher and the prices lower for comparable pieces, but that, thanks to the successful development of a system of interchangeable parts, repairs were much easier. To reinforce his argument, Favre-Perret related an experiment:

> I asked the director of the Waltham Company for a watch of the fifth grade. A large safe was opened before me; at random I took a watch out and fastened it to my chain... At Paris I set my watch by a regulator on the Boulevard, and on the sixth day I observed that it had varied by 30 seconds. And this is a watch of the fifth American grade – it costs 75 francs... On my arrival in Le Locle I showed the watch to one of our first adjusters, who asked my permis-sion to 'take it down'... After a lapse of a few days he came to me and said, word for word: 'I am completely overwhelmed; the result is incredible; one would not find one such watch among fifty thousand of our manufacture.'

His reporting of the success of the Americans

The Philadelphia Centennial Exhibition 1876 — opening ceremony.

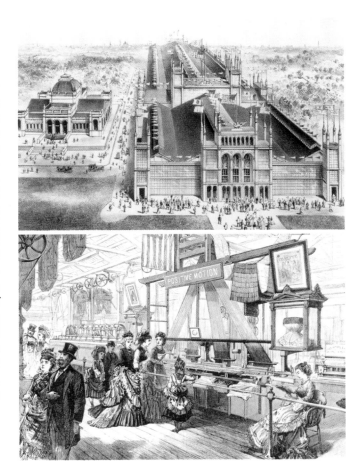

in achieving absolute interchangeability of parts was somewhat exaggerated, as he later admitted. It seemed that even they had failed to reach the stage where no hand finishing was required; that was not to come until well into the next century. The exception was the introduction of the cheap 'dollar watch' around 1900; hand finishing at that price was impossible, and firms such as Ingersoll simply binned sub-standard parts and replaced faulty watches. It was not until the 1930s that machines were developed that could work to the tolerances of less than 1 micron (a thousandth of a millimetre) necessary for producing truly interchangeable parts for jewelled watches. However, unlike the British who, with a couple of exceptions, let industrialized production pass them by, the Swiss took the American advances very seriously.

The International Watch Co.

By the time Favre-Perret was investigating American production methods, F.A. Jones, who had been a director of E. Howard & Co., Boston, one of America's leading watch manufacturers, had set up a watch factory at Schaffhausen in the far north of Switzerland on the German border. In 1869 he rented premises from a local industrialist and watch manufacturer, Heinrich Moser, who had met Jones earlier and was keen to promote his plans to bring American machine production to Switzerland.

The International Watch Co. (IWC) soon outgrew its original premises, and in 1875 a new factory was opened on the banks of the Rhine with a workforce of 196, producing high-grade American-style models. A year later, due to sluggish sales, Jones was forced into bankruptcy and had to leave the company, which was taken over by the Schaffhausen Handelsbank and sold off to largely Swiss stockholders.

The new board appointed the American engineer F.F. Seeland as director; he was the sole foreign stockholder and had experience with both machine production and marketing; he was also, unlike Jones, a fluent German speaker. Seeland completed the remaining stock of the Jones movements, but decided that midrange three-quarter-plate watches would sell better in addition to the earlier full-plate 'Boston' models based on American designs.

Unfortunately, Seeland encountered the same problems as Jones in selling watches to already saturated markets in America and Europe; he did manage to export a quantity of IWC watches to Britain, but sales did not keep up with production. In desperation, Seeland resorted to some 'creative accounting' to attempt to keep the firm afloat, and in 1879 he had to make a swift exit to the USA to avoid arrest for fraud. After the inevitable bankruptcy, the company

Early IWC 'Jones' model B watch, c.1876.

Early IWC digital watch, 1885.

IWC hunting cased watch, 1920s.

IWC model C watch, c.1878.

IWC Mk 11 military model, 1948.

was taken over by the Rauschenbach family who continued in ownership for four generations.

The IWC factory in Schaffhausen did much to introduce the Swiss to American methods of machine production under the direction of Urs Haenggi, who joined the company in 1883 and stayed with them for fifty-two years. In 1883, electric power was introduced from a nearby hydroelectric plant, at first for lighting and electroplating, and later for powering the machinery. The factory had a narrow escape in 1944, when, as a result of a navigation error, it was bombed by an American aircraft. A high-explosive bomb failed to explode, and the firm's own fire brigade extinguished the fires resulting from incendiaries.

THE WRIST WATCH

The first true wrist watches appeared in the late nineteenth century. They were small watches set into jewelled bracelets; Vacheron & Constantin produced an early example in 1889. Various makers made such watches worn by women as much an item of jewellery as a timepiece; however, in 1912 the *New York Times* reported from Paris:

> The wrist watch ... is now the fashion of the hour... It is worn over here by women who have to work as well as those who play... it is the most useful piece of jewelry that has been invented for many decades. ... The watch hidden away in the belt, or turned face downward on the bust, or swinging loose from a chatelaine pin, was an ornament but not always a help. As it was usually under one's furs or topcoat in Winter, it was better to guess the time than to try to prove it.

During the second Boer War (1899–1902), some army officers also adopted the practice of wearing a watch on the wrist, and Mappin & Webb marketed a 'campaign watch' in 1889. Modern warfare often depended on precise timing of military movements, and the inconvenience of using a pocket watch, particularly on horseback, is obvious. One British retailer advertised that their 'wristlet watch' had sur-

Vacheron & Constantin bracelet watch, 1889.

vived the Battle of Omdurman, maintaining that 'desert experience is the severest test a watch can have'. The ever-resourceful Swiss soon spotted the potential for the new idea, and in 1903 Dimier Freres & Cie patented a wrist watch with what became the standard wire lugs.

The Rolex Watch Company

The London-based watch company Wilsdorf & Davis, later to become the Rolex Watch Company, contracted with the Swiss maker Aegler to manufacture a line of wrist watches; they brought out their first Rolex wrist watch in 1910. The company was founded by Hans Wilsdorf, a German who as a young man was employed as an English correspondent and clerk with a Swiss watch manufacturer in La Chaux-de-fonds. He moved to London in 1905 and set up in partnership with Alfred Davis, trading as Wilsdorf and Davis; the company registered the brand name 'Rolex' in 1908. The firm imported Swiss movements made by Herman Aegler and had the cases made in England by several makers, including A.L. Dennison.

In 1914 a Rolex watch was awarded a class A precision certificate by Kew Observatory, a considerable coup as this award was previously confined to large deck watches, and proved that a wrist watch was capable of a high level of accuracy. The popularity of wrist watches really took off with World War I when the 'trench watch' became standard equipment, first for artillery officers and then more widely.

After the war, the Rolex Watch Company moved to Switzerland, where Wilsdorf registered the firm as Montres Rolex SA, and in 1920 began manufacturing watches in a new factory in Geneva. It was here that Wilsdorf produced the first waterproof watch, the 'Oyster', in 1926. Rolex outlets displayed these watches

submerged in aquarium tanks in their windows to convince wary customers of its qualities. A year later, the British swimmer, Mercedes Gleitze swam the channel with an Oyster watch on a chain around her neck; Wilsdorf immediately took the entire front page of the *Daily Mail* to advertise the achievement.

In 1931 Rolex introduced their first automatic movement. Various other makers in the late 1920s, including the inventor of the modern automatic watch, John Harwood, had attempted to market self-winding models, but none survived the recession of the early 1930s. The 'Rolex Perpetual', however, was highly successful, and went unchallenged for over a decade.

1910 Rolex wristwatch.

The first Rolex Oyster model, 1926.

American airman wearing a wristwatch, 1918.

Mercedes Gleitze, cross-channel swimmer.

Antoine LeCoultre

One of the Swiss pioneers of factory production was Antoine LeCoultre (1803–1881); he was descended from French Huguenots who had settled in the Vallée de Joux. He opened his first workshop in Le Sentier, where his ancestors had lived since the sixteenth century. In addition to making watches, he invented several new machines, including the 'millionomètre' – the first instrument to measure down to a micron. In 1866, together with his son, he set up the area's first watch factory, and by 1870 they employed a staff of 500, making a wide range of movements including chronographs and repeaters.

The 'Tank'

In 1907 the firm's long association with the Paris jeweller Cartier began; the French watchmaker Edmond Jaeger, who had an exclusive contract with Cartier to supply movements, in turn contracted LeCoultre to manufacture them. This collaboration led to the creation of one of the most iconic of all watch designs: the 'Tank'. It was designed by Louis Cartier in 1917 and was said to have been inspired by the Renault tanks Cartier had seen on the Western Front. The prototype was presented to General John Pershing of the American Expeditionary

Celebrity sponsorship.

Force in 1918, and the watch went into production in 1919 when just six watches were made, all of which sold very quickly.

Production rose slowly during the 1920s, but rarely exceeded 100 per annum; then from the 1960s the watch was taken up by celebrities such as Jackie Kennedy, Andy Warhol and Princess Diana, and it took off.

The 'Reverso'

In 1930 a Group of British polo players in India contacted César de Tray, a watch dealer, to create a watch that would survive their sport's rigours. He approached LeCoultre, who designed a new case that would protect the fragile watch glass. The new model, now named the 'Reverso', went into production in 1931. In the late 1930s, the company acknowledged the link with the firm of Jaeger and became Jaeger LeCoultre (JLC), although in the USA they continued to be marketed as LeCoultre.

The Reverso sold well through the 1930s, but after World War II the Art Deco look was out of fashion, and production ceased. However, in 1972 Giorgio Corvo, an Italian dealer, purchased 200 unused Reverso cases from the

Original Cartier 'Tank', 1919.

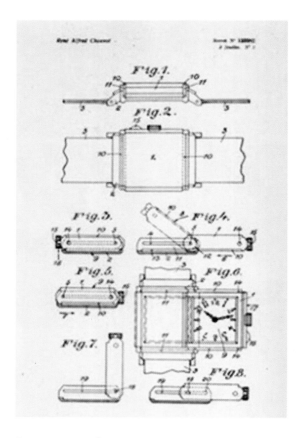

Reverso patent drawings.

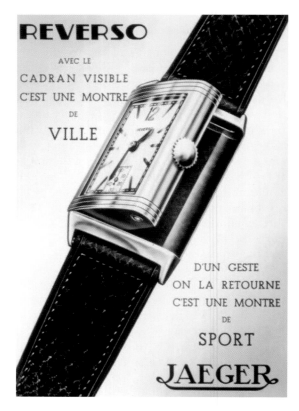

Reverso advertisement.

Omega advertisement, 1895.

manufacturer and had movements fitted; they were a great success and soon sold out. JLC eventually took the hint and revived the watch in 1982 with a range of mechanical and quartz movements; in its many versions, the watch soon became their most successful product.

THE OMEGA WATCH COMPANY

The origins of the Omega Watch Company go back to 1848 when Louis Brandt founded La Générale Watch Co. in La Chaux-de-Fonds; his modest *fabrique* prospered, concentrating on assembling and finishing the *ébauches* produced in the region. The firm prospered, and in 1885 moved to a new factory in Bienne, and in the 1890s, the brothers Louis Paul and César Brandt introduced an advanced mechanized production system. They began to manufacture complete watches under the brand name

Omega chronograph, 1932.

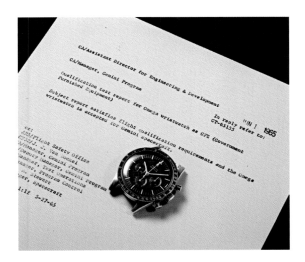

The Omega Speedmaster is approved for manned space flights.

Omega; in 1903 the brand was separated from La Générale and began trading as the Omega Watch Co.

Under the management of Paul-Émile Brandt, the new company was now employing a workforce of 800, producing 240,000 watches per annum. During World War I, both the Royal Flying Corps and the US Army approved Omega as suppliers of combat watches. In 1932

they became the official timekeeper of the Olympic Games.

In 1965 the Omega Speedmaster chronograph was approved by NASA for use on the Gemini space programme, and was later worn by the Apollo astronauts on the moon.

Omega and Rolex Rivalry

Omega and Rolex were always rivals in the luxury watch market. Rolex tended to be more conservative, concentrating on developing its traditional movements, whereas Omega was more progressive, constantly producing new models. In the event, when the 'quartz crisis' of the 1970s caused chaos in the Swiss watch industry, it was Omega that made the disastrous decision to try to compete in the electronic watch market; however, their high-priced models failed to find a place in a market dominated by the Japanese. Rolex, despite a brief flirtation with quartz movements, wisely concentrated on their traditional models and survived as an independent maker.

Société Suisse pour l'Industrie Horlogère (SSIH), the parent company of several manufacturers including Tissot and Omega, collapsed during the 1970s, with sales dropping from 12.4 million watches to 1.9 million.

In 1980 they were bailed out by the Swiss banks, together with the ASUAG Group (Allgemeine Gesellschaft der Schweizerischen Uhrenindustrie AG), which included Longines and the main ébauches makers, such as ETA (the manufacturing division of the Eterna Watch Co.), and A. Schild, who supplied many popular brands with movements. Nicholas Hayak, who had long experience in advising watch manufacturers on restructuring their businesses, proposed the merging of ASUAG and SSIH. The new group, Societe de Microelectronique et d'Horologerie (SMH), which became the largest watch manufacturer in the world, was founded in 1983: Hayak became the chairman, and CEO in 1985.

Now that he was in control of the group, which was later renamed Swatch, Hayak set about a radical reorganization of the industry: all manufacturing and development was now centred on the ETA plant in Grenchen, and soon the factories of once famous names such as Omega and Longines were closed down. The economies of scale achieved by the new Swatch Group for both mechanical and quartz movements enabled huge resources to be put into marketing what were essentially similar products. Thus the different brands were no longer autonomous enterprises – they became part of a carefully structured selling operation aimed at different sectors of the market from luxury brands down to the humble, but immensely successful, plastic Swatch watch.

A few manufacturers at the luxury end of the market have maintained their independence: Patek Phillippe is an example of a small firm, founded in Geneva in 1839, that concentrates exclusively on high quality, and specializes in complicated watches, producing just a few thousand watches each year. The financial crisis in the 1930s forced the sale of the company to the Stern family, who after World War II increased annual production to around 20,000 watches by the year 2000, and successfully found a niche in the high-end watch market.

A new group in the luxury market was established in 1988 by the owners of the tobacco giant BAT, the Ruppert family, as a way of diversifying its business. Named the 'Richmond Group', they took over several brands including Vacheron & Constantin, Jaeger LeCoultre and IWC (the International Watch Co.).

SWISS BUDGET WATCHES

Whilst better known for its luxury brands, the Swiss did not neglect the production of cheap, mass-produced watches. George Roskopf (1812–1899) developed a new version of the lever escapement, the 'pin lever' (*see* Part I), which he incorporated into a very simple movement that could be cheaply produced. In 1867 he started marketing the watches in plain nickel cases with cardboard dials for less than a working man's week's wages.

The watches, called the 'Proletarian', sold well; however, as Switzerland had no patents at that time, Roskopf's design was swiftly copied in both Switzerland and America, where the Waterbury company, and later Ingersoll, sold their 'dollar watch' in vast numbers. Pin-lever watches of all kinds were produced in Switzerland until the 1970s, when quartz watches took over the budget sector. Makers included Bettlach and BFG Baumgartner. One of the last makers producing jewelled pin-lever watches was Oris.

Roskopf pin-lever watch, late nineteenth century.

Oris pin-lever watch, 1960s.

PART V:
THE AMERICAN WATCH INDUSTRY

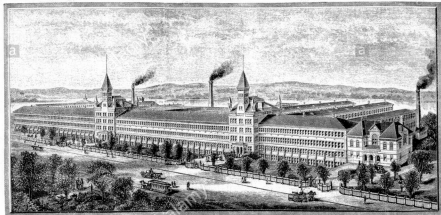

Waltham factory.

Chapter 21
The Origins of the American Watch Industry

The first watches produced in America were likely to have been finished mostly by English settlers, together with a few Europeans who brought their skills to the colony in the mid-eighteenth century. Most complete watches sold would have been imported from England or France. However, the Jefferson Embargo Act of 1807, which more or less cut off imports from Britain and France, created a demand for home-produced watches and clocks.

The first well-documented watchmaker working in the USA was Luther Goddard (1762–1842) of Shrewsbury, Massachusetts. His family were farmers who supported themselves during the winter by clockmaking. In 1809 he began making watches with his two sons, and took on apprentices as well as hiring several English watchmakers who had come to America during the Revolution as soldiers. They were essentially standard English verge watches; the specialist parts were purchased from Boston dealers who imported them from England. These were made in the same way as English watches, using the same, simple, hand-operated machinery as craftsmen in Lancashire across the Atlantic. The larger parts and cases were made and the watches finished in Goddard's workshop. It is believed that 530 watches were made in this way before production ceased in 1817, when the importation of cheaper European watches forced him out of business.

THE FIRST INDUSTRIALISTS

The origins of factory production in the American watch industry can be traced back to the early domestic production of simple wooden 'shelf clocks' in Connecticut in the late eighteenth century. The parts for these were made as much as possible from local materials, with a large number of wooden parts.

Aaron L. Dennison

Now recognized as the founder of the American watch industry, Aaron Lufkin Dennison (1812–1895) came from an industrious Maine family with roots in the colony going back to 1690, when George Dennison, who had been pressed into the British navy, settled in Annisquam, Massachusetts. Aaron was born into a shoemaking branch of the family in Freeport, and in an effort to better himself he moved to Brunswick to learn the clockmaking trade.

Luther Goddard watch, c.1810.

ELI TERRY

Born in South Windsor, Connecticut in 1772, Terry was apprenticed to Daniel Burnap. In 1792 he set up as a clockmaker and repairer, and eventually settled in Plymouth. Terry soon introduced water-powered milling machines and lathes to increase production, and devised machinery to make clock parts that were more or less identical in large numbers. This speeded up production considerably, and in 1806 he signed a contract to build 4,000 clock movements with interchangeable parts; it is claimed that these clocks were the first mass-produced machines made with interchangeable parts. By the time he retired in 1833 he had patented several of his inventions; his simple and affordable thirty-hour clocks sold in large numbers, and were quickly imitated by competitors.

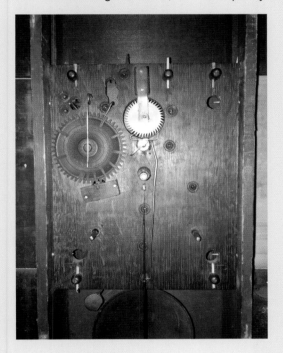

Clock movement, Eli Terry.

Eli Terry shelf clock, 1825.

At twenty-one, after completing his apprenticeship, he travelled to Boston to develop his skills in watchmaking, gaining employment at Jones, Lows & Ball under the supervision of Jubal Howe, who had been one of the apprentices in Luther Goddard's workshop.

Seeking to improve his skills further, he travelled to New York, returning to Massachusetts in 1839, establishing himself in the watch tools and materials business in Boston. As part of his business, he imported tags and boxes for the jewellery trade from France: ever with an eye for enterprise, he thought these might be made locally. After he had contrived the simple machinery necessary for the new business, he arranged for members of his family to take over production at their farm in Brunswick. Inspired by earlier attempts to manufacture watches by Henry Pitkin and visits to the new Springfield Armoury where guns were made with interchangeable parts, he dreamed of establishing a watch manufactory along similar lines. However, without influence or capital, his plans remained just that for the next ten years.

Aaron L. Dennison.

Edward Howard.

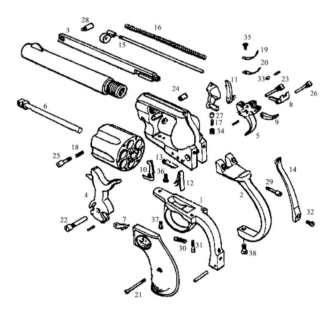

Colt revolver with interchangeable parts.

The Howard–Dennison Watch Factory

Edward Howard was a successful businessman and manufacturer of scales and weights; his firm had won a government contract to supply 40,000 balances for the new American postal service. He had also dabbled in the manufacture of clocks, sewing machines, leather-working machinery and fire engines. With that kind of experience and access to capital, Howard became a target for the ambitious Dennison, and in 1849 the two reached an agreement to set up a watch factory with funds supplied by Howard and his father-in-law Samuel Curtis.

Dennison left Howard to start organizing factory space in Roxbury, whilst he left for England to study British watchmaking techniques and locate sources of raw materials for the new enterprise. He returned in 1850 and started experimenting with designs for English-style watches with the new lever escapement, producing an eight-day watch in 1852. Just seventeen eight-day watches were made under the name of 'Howard, Davis & Dennison' (David P. Davis was a partner in the new firm). Dennison soon realized that this watch was over-ambitious, as eight-day watches were very difficult to make and tended to be unreliable.

tolerances as small as one five-thousandth of an inch. These machines needed constant attention and adjustment by highly skilled technicians; even so, the rejection rate of parts was always high. This could be mitigated to some extent by sorting parts into batches, such as separating wheels with pivots a little over or under size; these could then be matched to jewels with holes that fitted.

The Warren Watch

It took three years, with the use of English-made jewels, to get to the stage of producing

The watches, made with twin spring barrels, did not perform well enough to justify quantity production.

Ever the pragmatist, he realized that rather than going it alone, he needed to gather a team of specialists in the many different skills needed in the production of a successful watch. He did not hesitate to send his employees to England to learn difficult techniques such as gilding and dial making.

New machines were imported from England for making and finishing wheels and pinions; however, to achieve their vision of factory production, Dennison had to develop much new specialized machinery from scratch. A team of technicians was assembled with experience in machine production, including an ex-employee of the Springfield armaments factory and a few recruits from England. The task of producing interchangeable parts with the small tolerances required for watches was daunting, far more demanding than those for the clock or armament industries. Howard later wrote:

> If I had been able to foresee the trials and difficulties, I would never have started. Millions of dollars couldn't get me to do it again! Mr Dennison gave all his time and energy to this business, and he was determined to succeed, to realise his life's ambition.

Dennison's early machines were based on those already in use in European workshops, together with new measuring devices to check parts with

Thirty-hour watch signed 'Warren Boston', 1853.

their first batch of 100 thirty-hour watches in 1853 under the name of the 'Warren Mfg Co'. This was a paltry number by the standards of the early Swiss manufactories, but by heroic and unstinting effort, and despite constant problems of finance, early difficulties were overcome, and production increased rapidly.

The Warren watch was similar in construction to those being produced in large quantities in Liverpool and nearby Prescot in Lancashire, with the exception that it omitted the fusee. This was a considerable simplification, as the mainspring barrel geared directly with the centre wheel. This type of watch, known as a 'going barrel', became the standard design for future production in America, and was later taken up by the Swiss industry. English watchmakers stubbornly stuck to the older fusee design, a conservative attitude that contributed to the demise of English watch manufacturing after World War I.

A good deal of new machinery was developed for the production of the first batch of Warren watches, and a further 900 were made under the name of Samuel Curtis. These watches, which sold for around $40, were in no way an advance on their English prototypes in terms of timekeeping or reliability; however, they had more or less interchangeable parts and were much easier to produce and service than European watches.

The Factory Expands

It was clear to Dennison that the factory of the newly named Boston Watch Company would soon be too small. Land along the River Charles in Waltham was purchased, and a modern factory constructed there – the first factory to be built from concrete in America. It was ready for occupation in what to us seems an incredibly short period of time, a little over one year, in 1854.

The new factory employed about 100 workers and aimed to produce ten watches per day, although that target was rarely reached. Dennison's connections in the jewellery trade made the retailing of this quantity of watches possible, and a range of models with between seven and fifteen jewels was offered, signed variously C.T. Parker, Dennison, Howard & Davis, and P.S. Bartlett. However, things did not go as smoothly as hoped, and a business recession in 1856 threatened the firm with bankruptcy; to avoid closure, Dennison took to the road to gather promises of new financing for the fledgling company. After much horse-trading and scheming a new backer, the firm of Robins and Appleton, a New York watch wholesaler, was found, and was persuaded to invest $56,000 into the new business.

The American Watch Company

Royal Robins, now the majority shareholder, had faith in the new American watch, and saw that producing watches of standard sizes with interchangeable parts would give them the advantage over Euro-

The new Waltham watch factory in 1857.

Waltham factory, 1870.

pean imports. Denni-son, whose expertise was essential, was kept on as factory superintendent. In order to keep their jobs during the recession, the other employees agreed to a 50 per cent pay cut. A cheaper watch was designed, and in 1859 the company name was changed to the 'American Watch Company' (it was changed again in 1885 to the 'American Waltham Watch Company').

Robins now owned 85 per cent of the shares in the new company, and after the recession ended, the firm prospered and he began a programme of expansion. Dennison, now simply an employee of the firm, proved a difficult man to get on with, and with war approaching in the early 1860s he pressed for the production of a new, still cheaper watch, which he believed would sell well to soldiers. Robins disagreed, and eventually forced Dennison out of the company.

Rivals: E. Howard & Company

At the time of the sale of the Waltham factory to Robins, Charles Rice, who had put up some of the original capital for the factory – and thus had a share in the business – removed some of the watch material and machinery back to the old Roxbury factory. With the help of Dennison's ex-partner Edward Howard and fifteen of the Waltham employees, he set up as a rival to the American Watch Company. They began finishing old Boston Watch Company parts under the name of E. Howard & Company.

The new firm concentrated on quality, and was soon producing watches that were superior to those from the Waltham factory, with temperature-compensated balances and a new,

faster beat gear train. The traditional English watch had a 14,400 train – that is, 14,400 beats per hour, or 4Hz; Howard increased the frequency of the balance to five beats per second, or 18,000 per hour: this increased accuracy and became the new American standard. It was later taken up by the Swiss industry as the universal standard, and lasted into the 1950s, when still higher frequency balances were adopted.

Other innovations were included, such as a new design of spring barrel patented by George

One of the first watches produced at the Howard watch factory.

P. Reed – another old Waltham employee: this design protected the gear train from damage in the event of a mainspring breakage.

In 1858 Edward Howard took control of the company, and the firm began trading as E. Howard & Company. From the outset, Howard's aim was to produce factory-made watches of high quality, rather than try to compete on price with his larger rival at Waltham. Apart from the 18,000 train and the new spring barrel, many other innovations were adopted – some more successful than others, including the whiplash regulator, which is still used in precision watches. The firm was the first in America to regulate watches for isochronism, temperature and position. It had long been realized that timing a watch in one position – for example, dial up – produced a different rate from dial down, and high precision watches are adjusted to keep time within certain limits in five, or even more positions.

The Howard watch company continued producing high quality watches of innovative design, producing around 100,000 watches by the early twentieth century, constantly striving to increase the precision of interchangeable parts by the development of ever more advanced machinery.

The Civil War gave a welcome boost to the watch market, as one of the few personal possessions a soldier could take with him was a watch; by 1865 the Waltham company had produced around 190,000 units, and Howard around 50,000. Two main types of movement emerged: full plate and three-quarter plate, both influenced by English designs. Later, Howard introduced a more advanced split-plate design, which, though more difficult to produce, made servicing much easier.

Howard watch, 1862.

Howard movement from 1902; note the whiplash regulator.

Typical Waltham full-plate movement.

Waltham three-quarter-plate design.

Howard split-plate movement.

The National Watch Company – Elgin

The success of the Waltham company encouraged several new watch manufacturers to set up in 1864, backed by capital from the jewellery trade. A Chicago watchmaker, John C. Adams, saw the potential in the fast-growing city, and with financial backing from a local industrialist and ex-mayor, he began setting up a factory in nearby Elgin, luring several key workers from the American Watch Company in Waltham with promises of high wages and land for homesteading.

John C. Adams.

Elgin watch factory 1869.

ABOVE: View of the Elgin machine shop, 1869.

The main problem in starting such an enterprise was the long period needed to develop new machinery for producing watches. It was not until 1867 that the first watches from the new National Watch Company – Elgin appeared; they were full plate, key-wind watches of similar design to those being produced at Waltham.

The new company thrived, and an early success was a high quality fifteen-jewel watch named the B.W. Raymond, which became popular with the railroad companies and was produced well into the twentieth century. The firm was well managed, and constant investment in new machinery and innovative designs resulted in Elgin eventually overtaking Waltham in production.

Early Elgin seven-jewel watch.

Elgin railroad-grade watch, c.1870.

Other companies founded in the 1860s included the United States Watch Company in Marion, New Jersey; the Hampden Watch Company in Canton, Ohio, and the Newark Watch Company, Newark, New Jersey; however, none of these firms survived beyond 1878.

Elgin railroad watch, c.1900.

Chapter 22
Watches for the Masses

The cost of Waltham watches in the early 1860s at around $40 put them out of the reach of the working man, who at the time was earning around $1 per day. In an effort to make watches more affordable, they introduced the C.T. Parker, a full plate seven-jewel model that sold for $20 in 1854, and, spurred on by increased demand during the Civil War, the William Emery three-quarter plate model in 1862.

As the Waltham company continued to develop ever cheaper watches to compete with new budget-priced models imported from Switzerland, they decided to separate them from their higher quality models. They branded them as 'Home Watch Company', and in 1873 the Broadway model was introduced, which retailed at around $10.

Waltham C.T. Parker watch, c.1854.

Waltham William Emery watch, c.1862.

Waltham Home Watch Company model, c.1868.

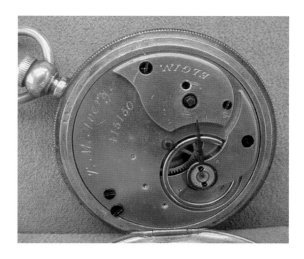

Elgin T.M. Avery watch, c.1870.

PIN-LEVER WATCHES

In Switzerland, George Roskopf (1812–1899) had designed a simplified watch that could be sold for around $6. He used a pin-lever escapement, which replaced the pallet jewels with steel pins (*see* Part I), together with a simple three-wheel train and large spring barrel; it had minimal finishing and a plain nickel case. In 1867 he marketed the watch under the name of La Prolétaire. By the 1870s Swiss Roskopf-type watches, still produced by traditional craft methods, were being imported into the United States in large numbers. Both Waltham and Elgin responded with new watch designs that

could be sold for $5–6; however, the goal of a truly cheap watch was still to be achieved.

THE 'DOLLAR WATCH'

A big breakthrough came from the clock manufacturing industry in Connecticut, where machinery had been developed to stamp parts from rolled brass sheet, greatly reducing production costs. The firm of Benedict & Burn-

Waltham Broadway watch, c.1873.

Waterbury duplex 1880s watch.

Waterbury with skeletonized dial — early 1880s.

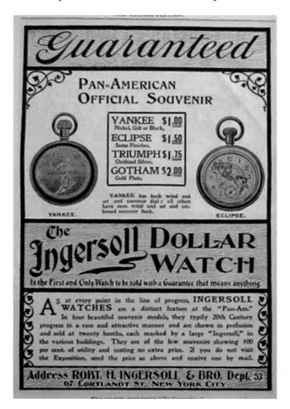

Ingersoll Yankee one-dollar watch.

ham, which later became the Waterbury Watch Company, made a large investment in a state-of-the-art factory with advanced machinery. They developed a radically simplified movement design that reduced the normal 150 parts of a conventional watch to just fifty-four. In 1881 the new factory was producing 600 watches per day, increasing to over 1,000. These watches sold in vast numbers for less than $3 each; however, by the 1890s other companies such as Ingersoll broke new ground, and the Ingersoll Yankee, introduced in 1896, sold for just $1.

ABOVE: *Production line at Ingersoll factory, early 1900s.*

LEFT: *Ingersoll advertisement, c.1900.*

Chapter 23
Upmarket Production

Alongside the development of ever-cheaper watches for the mass market, American manufacturers were determined to break into the European domination of the market in precision watches. The three most important firms of Waltham, Howard and Elgin led the way in developing machinery capable of producing interchangeable parts to the high degree of finish that characterized the best English and Swiss watches. We must remember that customers were not only interested in the external appearance of a watch, but were expected to examine the movements of the watches on offer. To suit the taste of the time, ever more elaborate damascened nickel finishes were developed, together with stem wind keyless models adjusted for variations in temperature and positions.

The American centennial celebrations in 1876, culminating in the Philadelphia Centennial Exhibition, put the latest products of the American factory system on show, and visitors were amazed by such wonders as Edison's telegraph, sewing machines and typewriters, together with the latest steam engines and agricultural machinery. The Waltham American Watch Company exhibited automatic machin-

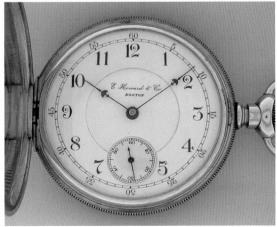

Philadelphia Exhibition 1876.

E.J. Howard watch, c.1900.

Cut-away drawing of Elgin twenty-three-jewel model.

at fifteen-degree intervals of longitude from Greenwich.

The major companies found, in the production of railroad grade watches, a useful new market for their high-grade watches, which up until then had been produced in small numbers as prestige products. Railroad-grade watches were generally characterized by dials with bold Arabic numbers, and were retailed at around $40 in a silver case. They were generally required to have a minimum of seventeen jewels, a lever escapement with steel escape wheel and double roller, an overcoil balance spring with micrometre regulator and to be adjusted for temperature, isochronism and five positions, accurate to within thirty seconds per week.

ery for the production of finely finished screws, pinions and balance staffs, and together with other companies, displayed their premium-grade watches. By then factory production had come of age, and American makers had proved that it was possible to match the best European watches in terms of timekeeping and finish in all price ranges from the simple dollar watch to premium-grade models such as the Waltham Riverside Maximus retailing at $180.

RAILROAD TIMEKEEPERS

As the new railroads spread across the continent, it became imperative to organize timekeeping, taking into account local times, particularly as most railroads were on one track, and it was necessary to pull a train into a siding to allow another to pass. Schedules needed to be strictly organized, and accurate watches had to be set with a company master clock to local time. Different companies had to coordinate their times, and various systems of achieving workable schedules were devised. It was at the instigation of the railroad companies that in 1883 it was agreed to adopt a standard system of time zones for the USA and Canada – five zones

Waltham railroad watch.

Elgin railroad watch.

PRESENTATION WATCHES

In the early years of the twentieth century watch sales were in the doldrums and Waltham decided that a dramatic gesture was needed to stimulate interest; the result was a new presentation grade of luxury watches. Up until then, Waltham's premium-grade watch was the Riverside Maximus retailing in an 18K case at $180; the new Premier Maximus had an introductory price of $250 and it featured, in addition to the usual refinements, a state of wind indicator (up-and-down dial) and was billed as the finest watch in America.

Not to be outdone, the Howard watch company, a firm renowned for high-grade watches, produced their Edward Howard model, which retailed at $350. This beautiful watch featured a gilded finish with blue sapphire jewels, a free sprung chronometer-style balance and wolf's teeth winding.

Other makers, such as Elgin, Hamilton and Gruen, also produced pocket watches of similar outstanding quality in the 1920s. Due to their high prices, these watches were mostly sold as prestige presentation items. In general, they failed in the aim of stimulating interest

Waltham Premier Maximus, 1908.

in the brand name, which it was hoped would improve sales of the more popular lines. American watch manufacturers had pioneered factory production and interchangeable parts, but their dominance in the late nineteenth century was

Howard advertisement, 1916.

shortlived. The Swiss learned the lesson very quickly and invested heavily in new machinery just at the time wrist watches were becoming popular in the early twentieth century.

The remaining American makers gradually fell behind the Swiss; companies such as Omega and Rolex were better at producing smaller calibres, and their elegant designs and high quality appealed to customers rather than the more stolid American pieces. In an effort to keep the Swiss at bay, ever higher duties were levied on imported watches; however, smuggling flourished and the Swiss authorities turned a blind eye, as they had towards smuggling for over two centuries. By the 1950s American makers such as Bulova and Hamilton were beginning to fit Swiss movements to their watches, and soon gave up production altogether.

Edward Howard watch, 1912.

PART VI:
LIST OF WATCH BRANDS

Chapter 24
Who Made Your Watch?

The bewildering number of watch brands too often gives little help in finding out who actually manufactured the important part: the mechanism behind the dial. The term ébauche comes from the French word for an unfinished painting or drawing. In the watchmaking industry it was applied to the basic, generally unfinished movement or parts supplied to another workshop or factory to be finished — that is, individual parts were polished, the movement was tested and adjusted, it then had the dial and hands fitted, and was cased ready for sale. The movement was generally unsigned, and the name, if any, on the dial might represent the retailer or the proprietor of a brand.

By the twentieth century the suppliers of ébauches often provided their movements fully finished, ready to be cased and sold under well-known and advertised brands, such as Rotary and Avia. Other well-known firms such as Brietling started out in the nineteenth century manufacturing their own movements, but later used ébauches from other makers. Even very exclusive firms such as Vacheron & Constantin, for instance, used automatic movements made by Jaeger LeCoultre and refinished them, adding their own name and calibre; both these firms supplied watches to up-market jewellers such as Cartier and Tiffany, to be sold under their brand name. The expensive marketing of watch brands is highly misleading, as the actual origin of the movement fitted to a watch is rarely disclosed, and even the term 'in house' should be treated with caution.

The so-called 'quartz crisis' of the 1970s almost destroyed the Swiss watch industry. The early, highly priced Swiss quartz models were swept aside by the Japanese makers Seiko and Citizen, who dominated the new watch market. Many famous Swiss makers failed and were absorbed into large groups with the financial muscle to market their brands effectively. Eventually, most independent manufacturers ceased production.

Once famous brands such as Omega and Longines continued to be marketed, but now were fitted with centrally produced movements from ébauches manufacturers, and the largest, ETA, came to make the movements, both quartz and mechanical, for most European watch brands; sometimes the ETA calibre is left on the movement, but more often this is replaced by the once famous manufacturer's name. The economies of scale resulting from this kind of reorganization greatly reduced the proportion of the final price of a watch represented by the movement, and this enabled a far greater budget to be allocated to marketing, which often exceeds the production cost of the watch.

The two main watch groups to emerge were the Swatch Group and the Richemont Group.

The Swatch Group: This Group was formed in 1983 from two older Groups: ASUAG (Allgemeine Gesellschaft der Schweizerischen Uhrenindustrie AG), which comprised the largest ébauches producers including ETA, AS and FHF, together with SSIH (Société Suisse pour l'Industrie Horlogère), which included Omega and Tissot. The CEO, Nicholas Hayak, was supported by several Swiss banks and a group of private investors. Originally named SMH (Société de Microéléctronique et d'Horlogerie), the organization adopted the name 'Swatch Group Ltd' in 1998. Manufacturing and research were centred in the ETA factory in Grenchen. They became the world's largest watch group, including the following: Balmain, Blancpain, Breguet, Certina, Endura, Flik Flak, Glashütte Original, Hamilton, Harry Winston, Jaquet Droz, Léon

Hatot, Longines, Mido, Omega, Rado, Swatch, Swiss Timing, Tissot, and Union Glashütte. ETA, the manufacturing arm of Swatch, also supplied movements to many other brands not in the group.

The Richemont Group: This group was founded in 1988 by South African billionaire Anton Rupert. It includes the following brands: A. Lange & Söhne, Baume, Baume & Mercier, IWC, Jaeger-LeCoultre, Panerai, Piaget, Ralph Lauren, Vacheron & Constantin.

LIST OF WATCH BRANDS

The following list of watch brands may be helpful. It has been checked against what sources are available; however, given the opaque nature of the watch business, it cannot claim to be definitive or entirely accurate. If the watch name you are looking for is not listed, it is probably a brand name rather than a manufacturer, containing a movement by one of the big ébauches makers, such as ETA or AS.

Alpina: Founded in 1883 by Gottleib Hauser, who founded the 'Alpina Swiss Watchmakers Corporation'. This was a union of independent makers who later developed in-house calibres of high-grade watches and chronometers. In 1901 the union registered the trademark 'Alpina' and adopted the red triangle emblem. Later watches used various ébauches, including AS, ETA, Felsa.

Amida: Manufacturer of pin-lever watches, both pocket and wrist models, including automatics and simple chronographs into the 1960s. Little information is available; it was probably founded in the early twentieth century. It was recorded in 1939 as producing ébauches in Grechen.

Angelus: Founded in 1891 by Gustav & Albert Stolz in Le Locle to assemble movements from other makers. From 1912 it specialized in chronographs. In 1942 it produced the first chronograph with date function, and the 'Chronodato' in 1948 with a moon phase. It

produced an alarm watch in 1958. It also made small clocks. It ceased production *c*.1980. The brand was relaunched in 2015.

Arogno: Makers of ébauches; founded in 1873 in Arogno in the district of Lugarno, where most of the workforce came from Porrentry. In 1899 the factory was rebuilt, and by 1918 was producing about 30,000 pocket-watch and wrist-watch movements per annum. It became a member of Ébauches SA in 1932. Also produced alarm clock movements. It ceased production in 1974.

Audemars Piguet: Founded by Jules-Louis Audemars and Edward-Auguste Piguet in 1875 in the Jura village of Le Brassus. Specialized in complicated pocket watches using local ébauches. Won the medal of honour at the Paris World Exhibition in 1899. In 1921 it created the jumping hour wrist watch, and in 1946 the super-slim calibre 9ML. It pioneered the modern tourbillon wrist watch. It claims to be the oldest independent family-owned watch manufacturer.

Avia: Established in 1887 by H.V. Degoumois in La Chaux-de-Fonds. After moving to Neuchâtel in 1933 the company registered the 'Avia' brand in 1937. The brand became well established in the medium price range using ébauches by ETA, AS. The Avia Watch Company was wound up in 2007 and the brand was acquired by the Fossil Group.

Bettlach: Member of Ébauches SA. It manufactured Roskopf and pin-lever movements. By 1967 it was said to produce over 7 million movements per annum.

BFG Baumgartner: Maker of pin-lever watches.

Bidlingmaier/Bifora: German maker founded by J. Bidlingmaier in 1900, with a factory in Schabisch Gemund near Stuttgart. It originally used Swiss ébauches, later manufacturing a range of wrist-watch movements including automatic and calendar models. These were sold under the 'Bifora' brand.

Blancpain: Founded by Jacques Blancpain in the village of Villeret near Amiens in 1735. By 1830 Émile Blancpain had built a new factory in Villeret. In 1859 they began production of complicated watches, and moved to the Swiss factory of Louis-Elysé Piguet in Brassus. In 1930 they took over production of the Harwood automatic watch. In 1961 they became part of the SSIH Group; their last watches were produced in 1975. In 1981 the brand was purchased by Jean-Claud Biver and Jaques Piguet, who produced luxury watches in a small factory in Brassus, with movements by Frédéric Piguet. In 1992 Blancpain was purchased by SSIH and was later taken over by the Swatch Group.

Brac: Manufacturer of a large range of pin-lever watches, including automatic watches and stopwatches.

Breitling: Founded in Saint-Imier by Léon Breitling in 1884. In 1892 the firm established a new factory in La Chaux-de-Fonds specializing in pocket chronographs. Léon Breitling took over the company in 1914 and developed the first chronographs with centre seconds hand and double pushers. The company used movements from several manufacturers, including Venus, Landeron, Valjoux and Lemania; in 1965 they commissioned Buren to produce the first automatic chronograph. In 1978 the company ceased production. The trademark purchased in 1979 by Ernest Schneider and Breitling Montres SA was relaunched in 1982.

Bulova: New York-based company founded by the Bohemian immigrant Joseph Bulova. In 1912 he opened a factory in Biel, Switzerland, producing a range of watches for men and women. Later he established a production facility in New York, moving in 1945 to new corporate headquarters near La Guardia airport, named Bulova Park. He introduced the 'Caravelle' mid-priced range in the 1950s, with movements by Citizen. Ébauches by many Swiss makers were used, including ETA, AS and Font. In 1960 the Accutron model was released, the first electronic watch, using a transistor circuit to control a tuning-fork oscillator vibrating at 360Hz. This was later taken up by NASA, and used both in instrument packages and as a backup watch on the Apollo mission. Bulova survived the 'quartz crisis' and was bought out by the Citizen watch company in 2008.

Buren: Founded in 1898 when the London firm of H. Williamson Ltd acquired Fritz Suter & Cie, of the Swiss town of Büren an der Acre, which produced both watches and table clocks. Williamsons expanded the factory, and from 1916 became the Büren Watch Co. H. Williamson closed as a result of the stock-market crash, and the firm was recapitalized and continued under Swiss management as Uhrenfabrik Buren AG. It was sold in 1966 to the Hamilton Watch Company, who transferred their US production to the Büren factory. It was taken over by the SSIH Group in 1971, and was sold off in 1972.

Buser: Founded in 1892 in Niederdorf Switzerland, Buser Frères & Cie SA went on to produce ébauches and finished watches both as Buser and Nidor brands. It was incorporated into the MSR Group in 1961, and was relocated to La Chaux-de-Fonds in the 1960s. It closed in 1978.

Certina (Kurth): Founded in 1888 by Alfred and Adolf Kurth in Grenchen. Originally sold under the brand name 'Grana', the firm adopted the brand name 'Certina' in 1938. It produced a large range of movements, including automatics, and marketed chronographs using Angelus, Valjoux and Venus movements. In 1983 it became part of the SMH Group, and later, as part of the Swatch Group, was positioned as a sports watch brand.

Citizen: Originated as Shokosha Watch Research Institute in Tokyo in 1918, using Swiss and US machinery and expertise. In 1924 it produced its first pocket watch under the name 'Citizen'. Suffering from investment problems, Shokosha went into partnership with watch importer Rudolphe Schmid, and formed the Citizen Watch Company, which began the production of wrist watches in 1931. After World War II the Citizen Trading Company was founded to develop the overseas market producing movements based on Swiss designs, and later developed a range of original calibres, including high beat models and chronographs.

In 1960 it came to an agreement with Bulova to supply movements for their Caravelle range; the arrangement ended in 1970. In 1964 Citizen opened the Tokorozawa Technical Laboratory, a research facility devoted to electronic watch research. In 1973 Citizen released the first quartz analog watch, the Quartz Cryston, the first of a highly successful range of quartz watches. In 2008 Citizen bought out the Bulova Watch Company. The company also has an in-house movement brand 'Myota', which became one of the major manufacturers of budget quartz movements.

Cortébert: The origins of this brand are obscure. The Cortébert brand was registered in 1855 after the Swiss village of the same name. It produced a jump-hour pocket watch in the late nineteenth century, and a jump-hour wrist watch in the 1920s. It made watches for Turkish and Italian railways. It produced a large range of movements, including automatics. Production ceased in 1970.

Croton: A US brand founded in 1878; owned by the Meermelstein family with a facility in Moonachie New Jersey. It used mostly ETA and AS ébauches. It has a plant in Hong Kong.

Cyma-Tavannes: The Tavannes Watch Company was founded by Henry Sandoz, who had produced watches in Le Locle from 1870. The new Tavannes Watch Co. SA began producing watches and specialized machinery in the town of Tavannes, in the canton of Bern in 1891. It formed a distribution deal with Shwob Frères of La Chaux de Fonds to supply watches for their Cyma brand. By 1929 Tavannes employed 2,000 workers, assembling 4,000 watches per day. It made a large range of movements, including automatics and small clocks. Production ceased in 1966, and the Cyma and Tavannes brands were acquired by the ASUAG Group. The brand was relaunched in 2008.

Doxa: Founded in 1889 by George Ducommun in Le Locle. In 1908 they produced an eight-day pocket watch used by the German army in World War I. Later, the brand used several ébauches suppliers including ETA, AS and Font. Taken over by the ASUAG Group in 1968, the brand was subsequently acquired by Aubry Frères in 1978; in 1997 it was purchased by the Jenny family of Bern.

Durowe-Laco: Founded by Ludwig Hummel in 1933, the Deutche Uhren Roh Werke in Pforzheim had links to Lacher & Co, which produced Laco watches. Durowe produced movements for Laco pilots' watches during World War II. The factory was destroyed by Allied bombing, and with the aid of the Martial Plan started production again in Pforzheim; by the mid-1950s Laco-Durowe was producing 80,000 movements per month. The firm was sold to Timex in 1959, which developed the first electric watch on the market using their patents. In 1965 Timex sold the company to the Swiss Group Ébauches SA, which continued production of mechanical movements until it ceased manufacturing in 1974. The Laco brand was relaunched in the 1980s but this attempt failed, and the firm became insolvent in 2009.

Ebel: Founded in 1911 by Eugène Blum and Alice Levy. It used ébauches from ETA, AS and Felsa. It became part of the LVMH Group from 1995 to 2003, when it was purchased by the Movado Group.

Eberhard: Founded in 1887 by Georges Eberhard in La Chaux-de-Fonds. Specializing in chronographs, it produced its first wrist chronograph in 1919, and in 1938, a chronograph with hour counter. It continues as an independent company; it has used Valjoux movements.

Ebosa: Maker of pin-lever watches.

Election: Founded by Alphonse Braunschweig in 1848 in La Chaux-de-Fonds. The brand name 'Election' was used from 1905. The company was taken over by Marvin *c.*1950.

Elgin: Founded in 1864 by Chicago watchmaker John C. Adams in nearby Elgin, luring several key workers from the Waltham factory. The firm was well managed, and constant investment in new machinery and innovative designs resulted in Elgin eventually overtaking Waltham in production. After World War II the firm used Swiss ébauches mostly by Font and AS. It ceased production in 1968.

Enicar: Founded in 1913 by Ariste Racine and Emma Blatt. It adopted the brand name 'Enicar' ('Racine' in reverse) in 1914. It used mostly AS movements, but also produced in-house models under the AR calibre. The firm became insolvent in 1967 and was taken over by Wah Ming Hong Ltd of Hong Kong, with distribution mostly in China.

ETA: Originally founded by Urs Schild and Dr Girard in Grenchen in 1856 manufacturing ébauches, and adopted the brand name 'Eterna'. In 1926 the movement branch of Eterna, ETA, together with AS and FHF (Font), founded Ebauches SA, which in 1931 joined the ASUAG Group and later absorbed many Swiss makers of ébauches and watch parts. ETA continued to be Switzerland's largest maker of ébauches, supplying movements for countless watch brands.

During the quartz crisis of the 1970s, both the ASUAG Group and the SSIH Group (including Omega and Tissot) faced severe foreign competition. The resulting restructuring of the watch industry involved the merging of the two groups; under the leadership of Nicholas G. Hayak, it eventually became the Swatch Group. All production for the Group was centred at the ETA factory in Grenchen, including brands such as Omega and Longines. ETA became the supplier of movements for most Swiss brands. Very few makers, mostly in the luxury market such as Rolex, maintained their independence.

Eterna: *See* ETA

Excelsior Park: Founded by Jules-Frédéric Jeanneret in Saint-Imier in the 1860s. It specialized in chronographs. Successors registered the name 'Excelsior' in 1902, and later added 'Park' to attract English-speaking buyers. Until

1983 the company produced a range of stop-watches and chronographs for Gallet, Girard Perregaux and Zenith.

Favre Leuba: Originally A. Favre & Fils: founded by Abraham Favre in Le Locle in 1792. This was a family business making ébauches. Collaborated with August Leuba, and established the Favre Leuba brand in 1815. It produced a range of watches, including chronographs in the 1920s and later automatic calibres. It remained a family business until 1969, when quartz competition forced its sale. It passed through several owners until the brand was acquired by Titan Company Ltd, part of the Tata Group; it specialized in sports models.

Felsa: Manufacturer of a large range of movements. Established in Grenchen in 1918, it joined Ébauches SA in 1928. It developed a successful bi-directional 'Bidynator' automatic winding mechanism in 1947. It was absorbed by the ASUAG Group, which later became part of the Swatch Group.

Fleurier FEF: Named after the town of Fleurier, which was a centre of watch part making. It became the Fleurier Watch Co. in 1915, and later joined Ébauches SA, which became ASUAG and was later absorbed into the Swatch Group. Its movements were used by many brands. It was later associated with the Chopard brand.

Font FHF: Originally Fabrique d'Horlogerie de Fontainemelon. It was founded in 1793 as Benguerel & Humbert in the town of Fontainemelon, manufacturing ébauches. The first factory was built in 1815; by 1876 it employed 400 workers producing 240,000 movements per annum. In 1900 the factory, under Paul Robert, was modernized, importing American machinery. It merged with Landeron in 1925 and joined Ébauches SA in 1926. In the 1950s it specialized in the manufacture of low-priced movements for Ébauches SA. Eventually it became part of ASUAG and was absorbed into Swatch Group ETA.

Frey Freco: Little information is available. Twelve calibres are listed. There are advertisements for watches in the 1960s for Frey & Co. Bienne.

General Helvetia: Founded by Louis Brandt in 1895, who set up the Omega Watch Co. The La Générale watch company produced watches under the 'Helvetia' brand, moving into wristwatch production in 1909 and trench watches in World War I. Later on, it produced a range of movements.

Girard Perregeaux: Founded by Constant Girard in La Chaux-de-Fonds in 1854; it became Girard Perregeaux in 1856 after Girard's marriage to Marie Perregeaux. Later models used mostly ébauches from AS, ETA and Font, although they pioneered high-frequency movements and early quartz watches. Relaunched with Ferrari in the 1990s as a luxury brand with tourbillons and chronographs.

Glycine: Founded in 1914 by Eugène Meylan, initially specializing in small ladies' movements; later it produced an automatic calibre, in production from 1931 to 1935; later it produced pilots' watches and chronographs. Ébauches from ETA, AS and Font were used. Eugène Meylan led a colourful life; he was accused of gold smuggling in 1947, and was murdered in Neuchâtel in 1955. The Glycine company became part of the ASUAG Group, and in 1972 switched production to US-manufactured LED models. It became part of the US Invicta Group.

Gruen: Dietrich Gruen & W.J. Savage founded the Columbus Watch Manufacturing Co. in 1876 with imported Swiss movements; later, in 1882, the New Columbus Watch Co. started manufacturing its own movements. In 1900 it became D. Gruen, Sons & Co., importing Swiss movements. Gruen wrist watches were introduced in 1908, and in 1917 moved to a new factory in Cincinnati. All movements were manufactured in a new factory in Bienne from 1922. By the mid-1920s it had become the largest watch company in the USA; it introduced 'Curvex' watches in 1935. After World War II some movements were made in the USA, but ébauches by ETA, AS and Font were also used.

The Gruen family sold their interest in the business in 1953, and the Swiss operation closed in 1977.

Hamilton: Established in 1892; the predecessor was the Keystone Watch Co., Lancaster PA. It was named after James Hamilton, founder of Lancaster County PA, where the new factory was built. Early production went to US railroad companies. It made wrist watches after World War I. During World War II all production went to the military, and the company produced marine chronometers and deck watches for the US Navy. In 1957 they produced the first electric watch. In 1966 they acquired the Buren Watch Co. and produced the 'microrotor' automatic. In 1969 they ended US production, and production was switched to the Buren plant. In 1972 production ceased, and the Hamilton brand was acquired by SSIH, later Swatch.

Hanhart: Founded by Johann A. Hanhart. It specialized in stopwatches from 1924, and later produced chronograph movements and time-measuring instruments.

Henzi & Pfaff/Hercules: Founded by Robert Pfaff in the late 1920s in Pforzheim using Swiss ébauches. After World War II it produced its own calibres, sold under the 'Hercules' brand. The company closed in 1972.

Heuer/TAG Heuer: Founded by Eduard Heuer in 1860 in Bern; in 1864 it moved to Brugg, near Bienne. It specialized in stopwatches and chronographs, and granted patent for 'oscillation pinion', later used in many chronographs. It was made the official timekeeper for the Olympic Games in 1920, 1924 and 1928. Later chronographs used mostly Valjoux and AS movements. The company's watches were worn by several Formula 1 drivers. In partnership with Buren, it developed an automatic chronograph in 1969. The company was sold to TAG, a Saudi-owned business group headed by Akram Ojjeh; the name was changed to TAG Heuer, and marketing was massively increased. As a result, the brand took a major place in the centre of the market, using both mechanical and quartz ETA movements. In 1999 TAG

Heuer was sold to LVMH Moet Hennessy Louis Vuitton SA, and luxury, limited-edition models were added to the range.

Ingersoll: An American company founded by Robert and Charles Ingersoll in 1882 as a mail order business. Their first watch, the 'Universal', was supplied by the Waterbury Clock Company, which later produced their 'Dollar Watch'; by 1910 they were making 3.5 million of these watches every year. The firm opened a British subsidiary to assemble and later manufacture parts for several pin-lever models. The company went bankrupt in 1921, and the Westbury Clock Company purchased it in 1922; it sold the British-based part of the company, which became Ingersoll Ltd, an entirely British-owned firm that imported parts from the USA. This became part of the Anglo Celtic Watch Co. in partnership with Smiths in 1947; a new factory was built in South Wales, where they continued to make pin-lever character watches, such as the Mickey Mouse and Popeye models, until 1969.

IWC International Watch Co.: Founded by F.A. Jones, who had been a director of E. Howard & Co., Boston; it was one of America's leading watch manufacturers. Jones set up a watch factory at Schaffhausen in the far north of Switzerland on the German border. In 1869 he rented premises from a local industrialist and watch manufacturer, Heinrich Moser, who had met Jones earlier and was keen to promote his plans to bring American machine production to Switzerland. The International Watch Co. (IWC) soon outgrew its original premises, and in 1875 a new factory was opened on the banks of the Rhine with a workforce of 196, producing high-grade American-style models. A year later, due to sluggish sales, Jones was forced into bankruptcy and had to leave the company, which was taken over by the Schaffhausen Handelsbank and sold off to largely Swiss stockholders.

The IWC factory in Schaffhausen did much to introduce the Swiss to American methods of machine production under the direction of Urs Haenggi, who joined the company in 1883 and stayed with them for fifty-two years. In 1883, electric power was introduced from a nearby hydroelectric plant, at first for lighting and electroplating.

From 1880 the firm was owned by four generations of the Rauschenbach family. It produced military models, including pilots' watches, and developed calibre 89 for the RAF navigators' watch. Their automatic model, based on calibre 89, won acclaim when it was introduced in the late 1940s. The 'quartz crisis' of the 1970s resulted in an urgent need for a capital injection, and VDO Adolf Schindling AG acquired a majority interest in the firm; in 1991 the company became part of the LMH Group, which included Jaeger LeCoultre and A. Lange & Söhne. The range was extended, and lower-priced watches with ETA movements were added, together with luxury top-end models. In 2000 the LMH Group was acquired by the Richmont Group.

Junghans: The company began as a clock manufacturer located in Schramberg, Baden-Württemberg, in south-west Germany. It started producing timers and wrist watches in 1927. After World War II it produced a range of watches, including chronographs; in association with Bauhaus designer Max Bill, it created a range of watches that influenced later designs. It was appointed 'official timekeeper' for the Munich Olympic Games in 1972. In 1995 it produced the first radio-controlled watch. In 2000, the watch division of the company was separated from the defence technology branch and was taken over by Egana Goldpfell Holding. In 2009 the company was acquired by Hans-Jochem Steim.

Keinzle: German maker of alarm clocks and pin-lever watches. In the late 1960s it started to produce electronic watches, including a solar-powered model.

Kurth: *See* Certina.

Lange & Söhne: Founded by Ferdinand Adolph Lange in 1845 at Glashütte, near Dresden. After his death in 1875 his sons Émile and Richard took over the business, building a new factory in 1873. The firm specialized in complicated watches and took out several patents, producing repeaters, chronographs and a tourbillon – the 'Jahrhunderttourbillon'. The company was patronized by German royalty, including Emperor Wilhelm II. During the twentieth century it produced both high-grade watches in Germany and mass-produced models with Swiss movements. During World War II some 13,500 high-precision military watches were produced. The factory was bombed by the Soviets on the last day of the war in 1945. In 1948 Glashütte came under Soviet control and the remaining watch factories were nationalized; the Lange name disappeared a few years later.

Following reunification in 1990 the firm was re-established as Lange Uhren GmbH, and since 2000 has been part of the Richemont Group, making around 5,000 luxury models per annum.

Langendorf Lanco: Founded by Johann Viktor Kottmann in 1883 in the village of Langendorf, Switzerland; it produced ébauches. Karl Kottmann modernized the factory in the 1880s, and the firm was named Landendorf Watch Co. By 1890 it became one of largest ébauches producers, employing a workforce of around 1,000. The brand of 'Lanco' was introduced in the 1950s. The company became part of SSIH in 1965. It ceased production in 1973.

LeCoultre/Jaeger LeCoultre: Antoine LeCoultre (1803–1881) was one of the Swiss pioneers of factory production. He was descended from French Huguenots who had settled in the Vallée de Joux. He opened his first workshop in Le Sentier, where his ancestors had lived since the sixteenth century. In addition to making watches, he invented several new machines, including the 'millionomètre' – the first instrument to measure down to a micron. In 1866, together with his son, he set up the area's first watch factory, and by 1870 they employed a staff of 500, making a wide range of movements including chronographs and repeaters.

In 1907 the firm's long association with the Paris jeweller Cartier began. The French watchmaker Edmond Jaeger had an exclusive contract with Cartier to supply movements, and in turn he contracted LeCoultre to manufacture them. The firm was rebranded as Jaeger LeCoultre in the 1930s, although it continued to trade as LeCoultre in the USA. They produced many iconic models, including the Cartier 'Tank', the 'Reverso', their automatic model, the 'Futurematic', and the 'Memovox' alarm model. The company was acquired by the Richemont Group in 2000.

Lemania: Founded in 1884 by Alfred Lugrin, who had worked for LeCoultre. The company manufactured ébauches as Lugrin SA, and specialized in chronographs and repeaters. In 1930 it adopted the brand name Lemania Watch Co., with its headquarters in L'Orient. In 1932 it joined the SSIH Group with Omega and Tissot. It produced many chronograph and timer movements, including calibre 1873 (Omega calibre 331), which was used in the Omega Speedmaster worn on the Apollo mission. It was acquired by the Swatch Group in 1999, but retained its manufacturing facility to produce movements for the Omega Speedmaster Professional and Breguet.

Longines: Founded by August Agassiz in Saint-Imier in 1832, and traded as Raguel Jeune & Cie. Later, Agassiz' nephew Ernest Françillon joined the firm and modernized production, establishing a factory at St Imier in 1867 with Jacques David as technical director. He took the brand name from the local name for the area, which was known as 'Les Longines'. The company produced award-winning chronographs and movements with keyless winding. From the 1920s a large range of watches, including chronographs, was produced. In 1983 it merged with SSIH, the factory was closed in 1986, and the brand was later taken over by the Swatch Group.

Marvin: Founded in 1850 by Marc and Emmanuel Didisheim in Saint-Imier; from 1895 the company concentrated on marketing to the USA. A new factory was opened in 1912, and the brand 'Marvin' was adopted. The company acquired the Election Watch Co. after World War II, and began using ébauches by AS,

ETA, Valjoux and Felsa. It ceased production in the 1980s. The brand was acquired by 'Time Avenue' in 2002, and relaunched in 2007 with ETA movements.

Mido: Founded in 1918 in Le Locle by George Schaeren. In addition to producing a small range of movements, it used ébauches by FEF, Peseaux and AS. From 1985 it was a member of the Swatch Group.

Moeris: A watch factory, founded in Saint-Imier in 1893 by Fritz Moeri and Julius Frédéric Jeanneret. They were involved in the early production and testing of Guillaume's new alloy 'Invar' in 1905, which revolutionized watch balance springs. It produced a range of pocket- and wrist-watch movements, became part of SSHI in 1931. It became part of the Reyville Group in 1974, and manufactured various replica pocket watches. Production ceased in 1978.

Movado: Established in 1881 in La Chaux-de-Fonds by Achille Ditesheim; by 1897 the firm employed eighty workers. It adopted the 'Movado' brand name in 1905. It produced a range of calibres, including automatics, and was noted for its innovative designs, including the 'Museum Watch'. It was purchased in 1983 by the North American Watch Corp.

MST Roamer Medana: The company was established by Fritz Mayer in the 1890s assembling watches; it produced its first movement in 1897. It formed a partnership with Johann Studeli in 1905, and Meyer and Studeli produced cylinder movements as MST calibres under the Medana brand. In 1917 they opened a new factory in Solothurn and began making lever movements, selling under 'Roamer' as their premium brand alongside cheaper Medana models. They produced their first automatic *c.*1950. They were incorporated into ASUAG in 1983, and eventually became part of the Swatch Group.

Nomos: German manufacturer, founded in 1990 by Roland Schwertner. An independent company with a factory in Glashütte, using in-house movements since 2005. In 2014 they developed a new version of the lever escapement known as the 'Nomos Swing'. They produce both manual and automatic models – unusually, they do not restrict the supply of parts, enabling any watchmaker to service them.

Omega: The origins of the Omega watch company go back to 1848 when Louis Brandt founded La Générale Watch Co. in La Chaux-de-Fonds; his modest *fabrique* prospered, concentrating on assembling and finishing the ébauches produced in the region. In 1885 the firm moved to a new factory in Bienne, and in the 1890s the brothers Louis Paul and César Brandt introduced an advanced mechanized production system. They started to manufacture complete watches under the brand name Omega. In 1903 the brand was separated from La Générale and began trading as the Omega Watch Co.

Under the management of Paul-Émile Brandt, the new company was now employing a workforce of 800, producing 240,000 watches per annum. During World War I, both the Royal Flying Corps and the US Army approved Omega as suppliers of combat watches. In 1930 the company merged with Tissot, forming the SSIH Group, and in 1932 they became the official timekeeper of the Olympic Games. SSIH continued to expand and absorb other companies, including Lanco and Lemania, the maker of a noted range of chronograph movements. In the 1960s the Omega Speedmaster chronograph with the Lemania 1873 calibre movement was approved by NASA for use in the Gemini and Apollo missions.

Financial difficulties in the 1970s, caused partly by the mistake of getting involved in quartz watch production, resulted in the sale of SSIH. It was eventually taken over by the Swatch Group, which closed the Omega factory in 1984; production moved to the ETA factory in Grenchen.

Oris: Founded by Paul Cattin and Georges Christian in the Swiss town of Hölstein in 1906; the company produced roskopf pin-lever pocket-watch movements. It continued to produce wrist watches with pin-lever movements, and by the 1960s was making 1.2 million watches per annum. After near collapse in the 1970s it became part of the ASUAG Group (predecessor of the Swatch Group), and concentrated on producing mid-range models with mostly ETA movements.

Panerai: Giovanni Panerai, a watch dealer in Florence, opened a shop there in 1860. His grandson Guido invented a gunsight, which he supplied to the Italian Navy from 1915. The firm also supplied the Navy with diving instruments, including watches designed and made by Rolex; production of these ceased in 1970. The company was relaunched in 1993 and became part of the Richemont Group, which repositioned it as a luxury brand.

Peseux: Founded by Charles Bernese in Neuchâtel in the early 1920s. It joined Ébauches SA in 1933, producing a range of ébauches for many brands. It consolidated with ETA, and production moved to the Grenchen factory in 1985.

(Henzi &) Pfaff/Hercules: Founded by Robert Pfaff in the late 1920s in Pfortzheim using Swiss ébauches. After World War II it produced its own calibres, sold under the 'Hercules' brand. The company closed in 1972.

Piaget: Founded in 1874 by Georges Piaget in La Côte-aux-Fées, supplying ébauches to various makers. After World War II the 'Piaget' brand was registered, and specialized in ultra-thin calibres including automatics. In 2001 a new factory was opened near Geneva producing high-end watches, including automatic chronographs and minute repeaters.

Pierce: Founded in 1883 in Biel, Switzerland, by Léon Levy and his brothers. It produced a range of movements including chronographs and pilots' watches for the RAF.

Record: Founded in 1903 with its headquarters in Geneva; by 1904 it employed 250 workers. The company was renamed 'Record Dreadnought Watch Co. SA'. It produced a range of calibres including automatics, and supplied watches for both the British and the German armed forces. It was purchased by Longines in 1961; some Record calibres were manufactured by Longines. It closed in 1991.

Recta: Founded in 1897 by Antoine Muller and Alcide Vaucher in Bienne. In 1898 the brand name 'Recta' was registered, and the factory was built in 1902. In 1917 the company was renamed 'Recta SA'. It produced range of calibres including chronometer rated models. It closed in the 1980s.

Rolex & Rolex Tudor: The company was founded by Hans Wilsdorf, a German, who as a young man was employed as an English correspondent and clerk with a Swiss watch manufacturer in La Chaux-de-Fonds. He moved to London in 1905 and set up in partnership with Alfred Davis trading as Wilsdorf & Davis; the company registered the brand name 'Rolex' in 1908. The firm imported Swiss movements made by Herman Aegler, and had the cases made in England by several makers, including A.L. Dennison.

In 1914 a Rolex watch was awarded a class A precision certificate by the Kew Observatory, a considerable coup, as this award was previously confined to large deck watches and proved that a wrist watch was capable of a high level of accuracy. After World War I, the Rolex Watch Company moved to Switzerland, where Wilsdorf registered the firm as Montres Rolex SA. In 1920 they began manufacturing watches in a new factory in Geneva. It was here that Wilsdorf produced the first waterproof watch, the 'Oyster', in 1926; and in 1931 Rolex introduced their first automatic movement, the 'Rolex Perpetual', the first really successful automatic watch, which went unchallenged for over a decade.

The Tudor brand was registered in 1926 to provide a cheaper alternative to the Rolex brand. Movements by various makers were used, including AS, ETA, Font and Valjoux. Some models were provided with the Oyster case, and diving models were added to the range. A range of in-house movements was introduced in 2016.

Rolex is one of the few watch manufacturers to survive the quartz crisis and remain independent; they did briefly get involved in quartz production, but wisely abandoned electronic mechanisms to concentrate on their traditional models. The company is owned by the Hans Wilsdorf Foundation, a private family trust.

A. Schild: Adolph Schild (1844–1915) began producing movements in 1896 in Grenchen, and became one of the largest ébauches makers in Switzerland by 1920. They became part of Ébauches SA in 1926, and joined the ASSUAG Group in 1931. They produced movements for many familiar brands until the quartz crisis of the 1970s. In 1979 the firm merged with ETA, becoming part of the manufacturing arm of the Swatch Group.

Seiko: The firm traces its history to 1881 when Kintaro Hattori, who had been apprenticed as a clockmaker, opened his watch and jewellery shop in Tokyo. In 1885 Hattori began importing Western timepieces and machinery, and in 1892 began to produce clocks; in 1895 his first pocket watch, the 'Timekeeper', was made under the name 'Seikosha'. In 1924 he changed the trade name to 'Seiko'.

The first wrist watch, the 'Laurel', was made in 1913; in 1929 Seiko became the official timekeeper for Japanese railways. By the 1950s the company was producing 3 million watches per annum, and an automatic model was made in 1954. To compete with the Swiss in the high-end market the 'Grand Seiko' was introduced in 1960. The firm was awarded the contract for timing the Tokyo Olympics in 1964.

The company had been involved in making quartz clocks for some years, when in 1969 they produced their first quartz wrist watch, the 'Astron'. By then Seiko had become a vast holding company manufacturing a range of products including printers and optics.

Smiths: Samuel Smith & Sons was established as a watch and clock retailer in 1851, and the firm prospered and opened several branches in London. By the late nineteenth century they had become London's major retailer of clocks and watches, selling a variety of English-made pocket watches, mostly from Lancashire and Coventry, with a small number of high quality pocket watches by Nicole Neilsen. Later, Swiss wrist watches were added to their range. In the early 1900s the firm began manufacturing instruments for the new motor-car and aircraft industry in partnership with the French firm of Edmond Jaeger, later taking control of the British branch of the company. The retail branch of Smiths was liquidated in 1932, and the firm concentrated on its growing instrument business.

During World War II, part of their factory in Cheltenham was retooled with Swiss and home-produced machinery to manufacture a small number of military watches alongside the much larger works making aircraft instruments. The expertise acquired during the war, and the assembly of a skilled workforce, enabled this branch of Smiths Industries to start work on developing a range of watches aimed at rivalling the quality of Swiss products – production began in 1947.

Throughout the 1950s and 1960s the Cheltenham factory produced a range of jewelled lever watches, including small ladies' models and later an automatic calibre; they were marketed under several names, including Smiths Astral, Smiths DeLuxe, Smiths Everest and Smiths Imperial (their top-of-range model). However, the Cheltenham watch production facility was never profitable, and had to be supported by the much larger instrument-making business; they ceased watch production in 1970. A plan to develop a quartz movement under the 'Quasar' name failed through lack of investment.

In 1945 the Smiths Group joined with Ingersoll to set up a new firm, the Anglo Celtic Watch Company with a factory in the Welsh village of Ystradgynlais. Here both Ingersoll and Smiths Empire pin-lever watches were produced with some success, capturing a large part of the British and Commonwealth market for budget-priced pocket and wrist watches. The factory closed in 1972.

Timex: The company was founded by the United States Time Corporation, the successor to the Waterbury Clock Company, to produce inexpensive watches with technology developed from wartime instrument production. The Timex brand was used for their pin-lever watches from 1950, and was widely distributed from mass-market outlets in the USA and world-wide. The Timex Corporation became involved in many enterprises, including electric and quartz watches, and in partnership with Sinclair, making the ZX series of computers until 1984. Later acquisitions, including 'Guess' and other brands, began to take over from the original brand from 2000.

Tavannes: *See* Cyma

Tissot: Founded in 1853 by Charles-Félicien Tissot in Le Locle, to finish and assemble parts from other makers in the region; in the first year the firm completed over 1,100 watches. Tissot's son Charles Émile succeeded in selling the firm's 'Savonnette' watch to the Russian empire. By 1918 the company was manufacturing its own ébauches. Tissot went into partnership with Omega in 1930 to found the SSIH Group, which became the largest Swiss producer until the quartz crisis of the 1970s: this crisis resulted in the failure of the SSIH Group, the brand eventually becoming part of the Swatch Group, when manufacturing was transferred to the ETA factory in Grenchen.

Unitas: Established in 1898 by Auguste Reymond, assembling movements from other manufacturers. Around 1906 the firm began producing its own ébauches in Tramelan in the canton of Bern. In 1926 Reymond purchased the Unitas Watch Co. and took over their brand name, joining the Ébauches SA Group in 1932. The firm produced a range of movements, including for pocket watches, which continued to be produced by ETA after the demise of the Unitas Co.

Universal: Founded by Numa Émile and Georges Perret in 1894 in Le Locle as the Universal Watch Co., an *établissage* assembling parts from other makers. By 1919 the company had moved to Geneva where it began manufacturing watches under the 'Universal Genève' brand; it became one of the leading makers of chronographs. A successful model in the 1950s was the 'Polerouter', which used the firm's new automatic calibre 215 'microrotor' movement. Like most Swiss makers, the firm suffered collapse

and the brand was acquired by Stellux, a Hong Kong investment Group.

Valjoux: Founded in 1901 by John and Charles Reymond in Les Bioux, specializing in chronograph movements under the name 'Reymond Frères'. They began production of their famous column-wheel movement, the calibre 23, in 1923, which stayed in production until 1974. The 'Valjoux' brand (from Vallée de Joux) was adopted in 1920. The firm became part of the Ébauches SA Group in 1944, and was eventually absorbed into the Swatch Group, when manufacturing was taken over by ETA.

Vertex: Founded by Claude Lyons in 1906 as 'Dreadnought Watches' using imported Swiss movements cased in England. In 1916 it began producing watches for the British armed forces. The 'Vertex' brand was founded in 1916. During World War II it was one of the firms that produced the WWW (wristlet watch waterproof) military model. It used movements supplied by Review/Thommens/Wittnaur.

Venus: Founded in 1923 by Paul Arthur Schwarz and Olga Etienne-Schwarz in Moutier, Canton Bern. The firm became part of Ébauches SA in 1928 and produced its first chronograph movement, the calibre 103, in 1933. Venus produced some of the finest column-wheel chronographs before moving on to low-cost cam switching models in the late 1950s. The firm failed and was taken over by Valjoux in 1966.

Vulcain: Founded in 1858 by the Ditisheim brothers in La Chaux-de-Fonds as 'Manufacture Ditisheim', taking the 'Vulcain' brand in 1894. It produced a range of movements, including the first successful alarm watch in 1942, the 'Vulcain Cricket'. The firm failed in the 1990s and the brand was sold to the PMH Group and relaunched in 2002.

Waltham: Founded by A.L. Dennison in 1850 in Roxbury, Massachusetts. After bankruptcy in 1857 the company was refinanced and became 'The American Watch Company': it pioneered machine watch production at its new factory in Waltham, Massachusetts, adopting the name

Waltham Watch Co. in 1907. Famous for its wide range of pocket watches, the company, like other American makers, was late to introduce wrist watches and never competed effectively with the Swiss makers. It ceased production in 1949. The brand continued in the 1950s using Swiss movements by AS, ETA.

Wittnauer: Founded in New York by Swiss immigrant Albert Wittnauer in 1872, importing Swiss watches, mostly by Revue and Thommen. During World War I it produced watches for the US Navy and early aviation units. Later it used movements by AS, Font and ETA. In 1950 the company was purchased by Longines, and marketed watches under both names. The brand was acquired by Bulova in 2001.

Zenith: Founded by Georges Favre-Jacot (1843–1917) in 1865 at Le Locle. He registered the 'Zenith' brand in 1900, and it produced its first wrist watches in 1915. It won various awards for precision, including first prize from Kew Observatory in 1929. It produced a range of movements, and in 1969 the first automatic chronograph, the 'El Primero'. In 1971 it was purchased by the American Zenith Radio Corporation of Chicago, manufacturers of electronic components, who ordered production to cease in 1978; however, the head of the chronograph studios, Charles Vermot, preserved machinery and designs, which enabled production eventually to resume. The Zenith brand was later sold to the Swiss Dixi Group, which collaborated with Ebel to revive production. Zenith ultimately became part of the LVMH Group, which positioned it at the top of their range of watches.

Further Reading

Baillie, G.H. (1979) *Watches, Their History, Decoration and Mechanism*. NAG Press.

Betts, J. (2007) *Harrison*. National Maritime Museum.

Betts, J. (2006) *Time Restored*. Oxford University Press.

Britten, F.J. (1987) *Britten's Watch & Clockmaker's Guide*. Methuen, London.

Cronin, John (2010) *The Marine Chronometer*. The Crowood Press.

Daniels, George (1974) *The Art of Breguet*. Sotheby's.

Harrold, Michael C. (1984) *American Watchmaking*. National Association of Watch and Clock Collectors, Inc.

Jones, Barry M. (2020) *S. Smith & Sons Ltd, The Golden Years*. Barry M. Jones.

Lands, David S. (1983) *Revolution in Time*. Viking.

Radage, Meinen & Radage (2016) *Through the Golden Age*. Three o'clock Publishing.

Rawlings, A.L. (1993) *The Science of Clocks and Watches*. BHI Longman Group.

Symonds, R.W. (1969) *Thomas Tompion, His Life and Work*. Spring Books.

Glossary of Horological Terms

action   Term used to denote the extent of the arc of vibration of the balance – how far the balance rotates on each swing; for example, a 'good action' is when the angle is large, say above 200 degrees.

adjusting   The act of regulating a watch to keep time. Adjusting can be in different positions, for example dial up, dial down, pendant up, and so on. High quality watches are adjusted in five or more positions and for variations in temperature.

arbor   The shaft or axle that carries a clock or watch wheel that often contains the 'pinion' or gear that drives the wheel; the balance arbor is normally called a 'staff'.

automatic winding   Device that uses the movement of the wearer to wind the mainspring of a watch.

balance   The controller or governor of a watch escapement. Usually in the form of a wheel that is made to oscillate, or 'vibrate', by an attached 'balance spring' and is maintained by impulses from the escapement.

balance cock   Bracket that contains the upper bearing for the balance, which holds the balance in place and to which the balance spring and regulator assembly are generally attached.

balance spring   Generally a fine spiral spring attached to the balance, often known as the 'hairspring'.

balance staff   Shaft or spindle that holds the balance, balance spring and roller.

banking pins   In the lever escapement, the pins on which the lever banks or rests. In a cylinder escapement a banking pin is attached to the rim of the balance to prevent 'overbanking', when the balance turns too far and locks the escapement.

barrel   Circular box containing the mainspring. It may be a plain barrel around which the fusee chain is wound, or it may have gear teeth cut into the periphery to drive the gear train directly – this is known as a 'going barrel'.

barrel arbor   Steel shaft on which the barrel revolves. It contains a hook to which the inner end of the mainspring is attached and is used to wind the mainspring.

beat   The 'tick' of a watch or clock caused by the action of the escapement giving the impulse.

bezel   Rim that holds the glass of a watch or clock.

bi-metallic   Two dissimilar metals, usually steel and brass, fixed together to form a strip that will bend with changing temperatures; it is used for the arms of a compensated balance, or the earlier 'compensation curb'.

black polish   Ultimate finish imparted to hardened or tempered steel, as opposed to a bright surface gloss.

bluing   Process of heating polished steel until the surface turns to a blue colour.

bow   Pivoted loop of a pocket watch case used for hanging or attaching a chain.

calibre   Name or reference number given to

the arrangement of parts of a particular movement.

cannon pinion   Pinion to which the minute hand of a watch is attached; it fits friction tight over the centre arbor and allows the hands to be turned.

capped bearing   Type of bearing with a cap, usually a flat jewel or 'endstone', which limits the 'endshake' or up-and-down movement of the wheel.

carriage   The rotating frame that carries the escapement of a 'tourbillon'.

chapter ring   Circular division of a clock or watch dial on which the hours and minutes are marked.

chaton   Ring or 'bouchon' into which a watch jewel is set.

chronograph   Watch with a means of recording a time interval, normally by providing a mechanism to stop a seconds hand and return it to zero.

chronometer   Term given to high-precision timepieces. Originally used to describe a timepiece with a 'detent' or chronometer escapement developed for navigation. Later the term was given by the Swiss to any watch that has passed prescribed tests and has been given an official timing certificate.

collet   Small metal ring, usually cut to allow it to fit friction tight over a shaft. Used to attach the centre coil of a balance spring to the staff, allowing adjustment.

compensation balance   Type of balance designed to compensate for the changing elasticity of the balance spring, which causes a gaining or losing rate. The rim of the balance is formed from a bi-metallic strip that is cut to allow the rim sections to bend in and out: this changes the rate to provide temperature compensation.

compensation curb   Bi-metallic strip, usually a steel and brass strip fixed together so that they bend with the change of temperature. Used to provide automatic regulation to compensate for the changing elasticity of the balance spring.

contrate wheel   Wheel with teeth cut at right angles to the plane of rotation. Used to transfer drive through 90 degrees.

crossings   Spokes of a wheel made by 'crossing out' a wheel blank, cutting away sections to lighten the wheel.

crown wheel escapement   Name given to the verge escapement when applied to a clock.

curb pins   The two pins attached to a watch regulator arm, which embrace the outer coils of the balance spring and can be moved to alter the effective length of the spring.

cylinder escapement   Frictional rest escapement developed by George Graham from earlier experiments principally by Thomas Tompion in the 1690s.

damascene   Originally described decorative steelwork from Damascus. In watch work, refers to complicated ornamental work on plates and bars.

detached escapement   Type of escapement in which the balance is detached from the escapement during its supplementary arc – that is, when the balance is not being given its impulse.

detent   Locking piece, usually a form of lever that locks a wheel by catching its teeth.

detent escapement   Detached escapement used in chronometers and other precision timekeepers. A detent releases the escape wheel to impulse the balance on alternate swings, leaving the balance free to oscillate without interference from the escapement.

dial   The 'face' of a clock or watch containing the hour markers; subsidiary dials can be included for showing seconds, date and so on.

draw   In a lever escapement after locking the pallets are advanced by a small angle (the 'angle of draw') to rest firmly against the banking pins, protecting against accidental release due to shock.

drop   The free rotation of an escape wheel after impulse has been given until locking takes place.

dumb repeater   Type of repeating work without a bell or gong: the hammer strikes a block, which can be felt when the watch is held.

ébauche   Watch movement as supplied by the manufacturer ready for finishing and casing up. Can be supplied in various forms, from very basic rough plates and wheels to fully finished movements ready for fitting the dial and hands.

end shake   The amount of up-and-down movement of a wheel between the upper and lower bearings.

endstone   Jewel fitted to form a cap to a bearing – the end of the pivot rests on it to reduce end shake.

engine turning   Sometimes called 'guilloché': a form of machine engraving used to decorate dials and cases.

English lever escapement   Name given to the ratchet-toothed form of the lever escapement favoured by English makers until the club-toothed form superseded it.

entry pallet   Pallet stone in a lever escapement on the advancing side of the escape wheel; the opposite stone on the departing side is called the exit pallet.

equation of time   The difference between solar time (as shown on a sun dial) and mean solar time (clock time). Due to the Earth's elliptical orbit around the sun the length of a day changes during the year. The average length of a solar day is called mean solar time (used by clocks); the difference in the two times can be calculated using an equation table that indicates the minutes to be added or subtracted to solar time to work out mean time. These are often seen on good sundials, and some watches have an equation dial that shows the difference.

escapement   Mechanism that controls the speed of rotation and thus the hands of a clock or watch, and at the same time provides the time controller (for example, a watch balance) with regular impulses to keep it in motion.

fob   Decorative attachment to a pocket watch used in place of a chain. A 'fob watch' refers to a small watch hanging from a brooch or clip.

front plate   Plate of a watch nearest the dial, as opposed to the top or back plate.

full plate   Form of watch with two main plates of similar size containing the wheels and escapement with the balance positioned above the top plate supported by the balance cock.

fusee   Spiralling grooved pulley of reducing diameter used to equalize the varying power of the mainspring as it runs down.

gilding   Process of covering base metal with a coating of gold. Before electroplating, items were covered with an amalgam of gold and mercury and heated to drive off the mercury, leaving a coating of gold.

gimbals (gymbals)   Form of universal joint used to maintain a chronometer in a horizontal position.

guard pin   In a lever escapement, the pin attached to the fork of the pallets, which in conjunction with the roller prevents the lever getting out of position.

hardening   Process of making steel hard by rapid cooling from a high temperature by immersing in water or oil. Generally accompanied by tempering, which is reheating to reduce the hardness to the desired level.

hog's bristle   Used before the invention of

the balance spring as a buffer against the arms of the balance, which gave some measure of regulation as it was moved towards and away from the centre of the balance.

Hooke's law   *'Ut tensis, sic vis'* — as is the tension, so is the force. Robert Hooke's fundamental law of springs.

hunter   Watch with a sprung cover to protect the glass; a half- or demi-hunter had an opening in the centre of the lid to enable viewing of the hands without springing open the lid.

impulse pin   Pin, usually a jewel, fixed to the roller of a lever escapement, which engages the fork of the lever and impulses the balance.

impulse roller   Part of an escapement attached to the balance, which transmits the impulse.

isochronism   An oscillating system, for example a balance, which can complete varying arcs of vibration in equal times.

jewelled   Term indicating that a watch contains bearings or surfaces that are made from jewel stones, usually corundum — sapphire or ruby.

karrusel   Form of revolving escapement, similar to the tourbillon but more robust and slower moving.

keyless work   Mechanism to allow a watch to be wound without a key.

lepine calibre   A form of watch movement in which each wheel is supported by a separate cock, with a cylinder escapement. The design allowed very slim pocket watches to be made.

lever escapement   Detached escapement invented by Thomas Mudge in 1754. During the nineteenth century it became, in various forms, the almost universal watch escapement.

lift   Refers to the angle of the impulse pallets of a lever escapement. The tooth of the escape

wheel traverses the incline of the pallets to impulse the balance.

locking   Action of arresting the rotation of the escape wheel after the impulse is given.

mainspring   Principal spring in a watch or clock. It takes the form of a strip of steel coiled into a barrel, which powers the mechanism.

maintaining power   Mechanism that keeps a fusee watch going whilst winding when the power is lost; a separate spring is engaged automatically during the winding operation.

mean time   The average length of all the solar days of the year. The usual time shown by watches and clocks.

minute repeater   Repeating watch that strikes the hours, quarters and minutes on the depression of a button or lever.

motion work   The gears that turn the hour and minute hands of a watch or clock.

movement   The complete mechanism of a watch or clock.

oscillation   A complete cycle or period, or repeatable alternation of a reciprocating body, for example a watch balance or clock pendulum.

overcoil   The upraised coil of a Breguet balance spring.

pair case   Pocket watch with two cases; the movement is fitted into one and this fits into the outer case.

pallet   The part of the escapement upon which the escape wheel operates and transmits the impulse to the balance or pendulum.

parachute   Shock-resisting device invented by Breguet to protect the balance pivots.

passing spring   A thin spring attached to a chronometer detent which flexes to allow the balance to pass in one direction and operates the detent on the return swing.

pawl   Detent or 'click' used to lock a wheel with ratchet teeth and prevent it reversing; it is held against the ratchet by a 'click spring'.

pendant   The part of a pocket-watch case to which the bow is fitted; in a wrist watch it refers to the position of the winding crown for timing purposes – for example, pendant up or down.

perpetual calendar   Mechanism that shows the date and adjusts for the length of the months and leap year.

perpetuelle   The name Breguet gave to his self-winding watches.

pinion   A small gear, usually the driven member of a pair of gears on a wheel; the teeth of this wheel are referred to as 'leaves'.

pinion wire   Extruded wire in the shape of pinion leaves, made by drawing several times through specially shaped dies. Sections are cut off to form the arbor and pinion of a wheel.

pin-lever escapement   Type of lever escapement where the impulse jewels are replaced by steel pins, also called the 'pin pallet escapement'.

pivot   The end of an arbor that is reduced in diameter to turn in a bearing.

pivoted detent escapement   Form of chronometer escapement where the detent is pivoted from an arbor instead of a spring detent.

poise   In equal balance. In horology it describes a balance that has an equal distribution of weight around the rim: it is then said to be 'in poise'.

positional error   The change in rate of a watch when it is in different positions. Precision watches are regulated generally in five positions: dial up, dial down, pendant up, pendant left and pendant right.

potance   A bracket, such as that which supports the lower balance pivot in a full plate movement.

push piece   The part of a watch case that is pushed to release a catch and open the case, also the pin which is depressed to engage a keyless work, or the piece to actuate a chronograph mechanism.

rack   Segment of a circle having teeth cut in the periphery, usually used to count out hours, minutes or quarters in a repeating or striking mechanism.

rack lever escapement   Type of lever escapement, where the lever has a toothed rack that gears with a pinion on the balance staff.

rate   The daily average timekeeping of a watch or clock.

remontoir   Device with a small spring that is wound by the gear train at regular intervals, providing constant force to the escapement.

repeater   Watch or clock that sounds the hours, quarters or minutes on demand by pressing a button or pushing a slide on the watch case.

roller   The disc attached to the balance staff of a lever escapement that contains the impulse pin.

shake   Term denoting the working clearance of a wheel, that is, end shake and side shake.

shellac   Resinous substance used to secure small parts such as pallet stones; it softens with heating and sets hard as it cools.

shock-resisting watch   Watch with spring-loaded bearings that protect the balance pivots from damage due to shock.

slide   Thumb-piece on the side of a repeating watch, which is pushed to operate the mechanism.

spotting   Form of decoration for watch or chronometer plates consisting of a series of circular rings.

spring detent   Detent in a chronometer escapement that is supported by a spring rather than the pivoted type.

stackfreed   Early device to equalize the varying force of the mainspring, superseded by the fusee.

staff   The arbor of a balance.

stopwatch   Watch with a provision for stopping the balance to note the intervals of time.

stop-work   Device to control the number of turns of winding of a mainspring.

stud   Block into which the outer end of a balance spring is fixed.

supplementary arc   The continued vibration of a balance after unlocking and impulse have occurred.

temperature compensation   Device designed to compensate for the effects of changing temperatures on the timekeeping of a watch or clock.

terminal curve   The curve applied to either end of the balance spring, intended to improve isochronism.

tourbillon   Revolving carriage invented by Breguet to carry the escapement and balance of a watch, which slowly revolves to counteract poising errors of the balance.

train   In horology, a series of wheels and pinons in a watch movement.

vibrations   In horology the term used to describe the swing of a pendulum or balance in one direction. The 'count' of a balance is generally described in vibrations per hour.

Index